SANDLER® SUCCESS PRINCIPLES

SANDLER® SUCCESS PRINCIPLES

11 Insights that will change the way you Think and Sell

David Mattson
Bruce Seidman

PEGASUS
Media World

Publisher
Pegasus Media World
PO Box 7816
Beverly Hills, CA 90212
PegasusMediaWorld.com

For further information, please visit www.sandler.com or call 1-800-638-5686

Sandler Success Principles: 11 Insights that will change the way you Think and Sell
© 2011 Sandler Systems, Inc.
ISBN, print ed. 9780982255421
Library of Congress Control Number: 2011945251

Cover Design: Alice Linesch
Interior Design: Lauraine Gustafson
Cassette tape image taken from "rpm vector collection" courtesy of John Politowski via www.vecteezy.com.

First printing: 2012

PEGASUS
Media World

Dedication

To David H. Sandler, whose profound understanding of human nature and keen devotion to the selling profession enabled him to not only create the most effective selling process, but also to raise the level of professionalism for salespeople throughout the world.

ABOUT THE AUTHORS

Dave Mattson is the CEO and a partner at Sandler Systems, Inc., an international training and consulting organization headquartered in the United States. Since 1986, he has been a trainer and business consultant for management, sales, interpersonal communication, corporate team building and strategic planning throughout the United States and Europe. Clients often describe his creative enthusiasm, problem solving and curriculum design as particular strengths that he uses to increase their companies' productivity and efficiency.

An early lesson for Dave in the sales process was the law of cause and effect: *If one works hard, then he will be rewarded. If one prospects, then his funnel will be full. If one has goals, then he will be farther ahead than if he had none.*

In 1986, Dave met the founder of Sandler Training, David H. Sandler, and fell in love with his training material. In 1988, he went to work for Mr. Sandler, and was eventually chosen to lead the company.

Bruce Seidman is the President and a partner at Sandler Systems, Inc. Bruce has been with Sandler Systems since 1983. He carries on the legacy his father, David Sandler, began in 1967. Bruce works closely with Sandler trainers to help them grow and continually stretch and improve, using technology to share best practices across the entire global team. Sandler Training's core strength lies in the growth and development of its 500-plus trainers, who live the Sandler Rules and Sandler Insights each day.

Contents ≪≪≪

Illustrations ≪≪≪

PREFACE
What Is Insight?

David Sandler once mentioned that he had decided to call his training programs "'sales' training" because that's what people would buy. David explained that what he focused on once someone became a client was what was "between his ears"—that person's thought processes.

David also said that success is not the result of strategies and techniques—although they play an important role—but rather an individual's attitudes and beliefs, fears and scares, perception of what's possible and what's not, and most important, self-image.

David Sandler established a number of "rules" showing how and when to implement the strategies and techniques of the Sandler Selling System® methodology. I explored and explained those rules in *The Sandler Rules, 49 Timeless Selling Principles and How to Apply Them*. In addition to those basic rules, Sandler also revealed a number of Success Principles—*insights*—that provided the psychological underpinning for many of those rules and corresponding strategies and techniques.

In this book, I'll provide you with an in-depth look at those insights. Some will make perfect sense to you. Some may make you uncomfortable. Some may make you smile. All will make you more successful . . . if you heed their message.

What Is Insight?

The dictionary definition of "insight" revolves around the concepts of *perceptiveness*, which is the ability to see clearly and intuitively into the nature of a complex person, situation, or subject and *self-awareness*, which is having a balanced and honest view of your own personality and often an ability to interact with others frankly and confidently.

Perceptiveness and *self-awareness* are certainly two indispensable skills for reaching high levels of selling success. Salespeople must have a keen sense of the nature of the selling situations they encounter. They must be able to investigate, analyze, and understand the prospect's needs, challenges, problems, and goals. At the same time, salespeople must be sensitive to the dynamics of their own interactions with the people involved in the opportunity, they must recognize the potential negative impact of those interactions on their own ego, and they must remain emotionally neutral throughout the encounter. As if all that weren't enough, they must act in an appropriate manner that doesn't damage the development of the relationship or the potential sale.

Clearly, it takes more than a pleasant personality, some product knowledge, and a little showmanship to pull all this off—in the sales arena or anywhere else.

It takes **insight**.

ACKNOWLEDGEMENTS

Thank you to the following individuals, without whose help this book would not have been possible. To the Sandler trainers around the world who give life and passion to David Sandler's work, and who have helped take the Sandler organization to heights and dimensions that David Sandler himself never dreamed possible. To the home office team, for your hard work and dedication to making Sandler the most innovative and effective training and consulting company in the world. To Brandon Toropov for your invaluable assistance helping us clarify and organize our thoughts. To Howard Goldstein, for your devotion to the integrity of David Sandler's message and your tireless work on this project.

PROLOGUE
Luck is preparation meeting opportunity.

There's an old saying: "If you want to succeed you've got to be in the right place at the right time." David Sandler, founder of Sandler Training and the creator of the Sandler Selling System, was fond of pointing out that that old saying came with a significant catch. Yes, it helps to be in the right place at the right time, *but you also have to know what you want*. Otherwise, you might be in the right place at the right time . . . and never even know it!

Picture two runners on a racetrack, blindfolded. One of them turns to the other and says, "Hey, do you have any idea which way the finish line is?" The other says, "No, I have no idea. But what do you say we start running anyway?"

Who wants to run that kind of race?

Neither one of those runners is going to win any Olympic medals anytime soon. If one runner "beat" the other, how would either of them know? It's an absurd situation, but is it really any more absurd than the way a lot of people choose to spend their adult lives?

> **Yes, it helps to be in the right place at the right time,** *but you also have to know what you want*. **Otherwise, you might be in the right place at the right time . . . and never even know it!**

1

If you were to ask a hundred people at random to identify where they want to be one, two, or five years from today—what "finish lines" they hope to have crossed in terms of income, relationships, contribution, or any other meaningful area of life—what do you think you would hear in response? My guess is you'd get a blank stare, double-talk, or a combination of the two from ninety-five of those hundred people.

Perhaps five out of those hundred people would be able to say, specifically, what it was that they wanted out of life within each of those timelines. Put those five people in the "right place," at the "right time," and, yes, great things can happen because they know exactly what they want, can visualize that outcome, and are ready to take action on that outcome. Once they know what they want, they can take advantage of the circumstances, relationships, and "coincidences" that support their goals.

The clearer you are about what you want in life, the luckier you will find yourself becoming.

You couldn't even *put* the other ninety-five people in the "right place" at the "right time." Why not? Because they don't know what they want! There is no right place! There is no right time! There is no finish line!

"Luck" really is the intersection of preparation and opportunity. The clearer you are about what you want in life, the luckier you will find yourself becoming.

Knowing what you want is an essential part of working any process, including the sales process. And *getting* what you want, once you know what it is, is what this book is all about. But there's a catch: you have to know exactly what it is that you want first!

Can You Claim the Prize?

As you read these words, there's a standing offer from Sandler Training of $500 in cash to the first individual who can deliver a

Ripitz. Let me ask you: Are you ready to step up and claim the prize for delivering that Ripitz?

Probably not. The $500 has been up for grabs since the early 1980s and no one has ever claimed it. The fact that no one on Earth actually knows what a Ripitz *is* may have something to do with that.

If we'd offered $500 to the first person who could provide us with a Christmas tree, or a copy of the Beatles' *White Album*, or a box of Cap'n Crunch, we'd have actually paid off the prize by now. But we asked for a Ripitz, and since no one knows what that is, no one can possibly attain the goal.

If someone were to ask you exactly what you have pictured for yourself one year from now, two years from now, five years from now, how clear would those pictures be?

The clearer the picture, the "luckier" you will be when you encounter the opportunities that support your goals. What do you see? Do you see a Christmas tree? Do you see a mint-condition, shrink-wrapped copy of the *White Album* from the vintage 1968 pressing? A brand-new box of Cap'n Crunch? A mansion in Santa Barbara, California? A 1965 Corvette? Six months off in Fiji?

> **If someone were to ask you exactly what you have pictured for yourself one year from now, two years from now, five years from now, how clear would those pictures be?**

Or, do you "see" a Ripitz? (Notice the quote marks.)

Goal setting gives you a track to run on.

Goal setting forces you to set priorities.

Goal setting separates reality from wishful thinking.

Goal setting makes you responsible for your own life. It forces you to define and establish your own value system.

Unfortunately, most people spend more time planning a two-week vacation than they do planning their lives. That's a tragedy, isn't it?

Beyond the Ripitz

Guess what? You can't possibly win the Ripitz bet. How about trying another?

This book is designed to help you eliminate internal obstacles so you can get closer to your goals. But at the end of the day, you won't be able to get any closer to your goals *if you have no idea what your goals are.*

> Ask yourself: Would you rather be one of the five people with a plan . . . or one of the ninety-five people without a plan?

Most people have wimpy goals or no goals at all. Why is that? In part, it's because they've convinced themselves, over a period of years, that goal setting is a pointless, useless, and boring exercise. *If we are not careful, we can convince ourselves of this and make it the operating reality in our lives.* That operating reality makes us one of the ninety-five people wearing blindfolds we could remove with five seconds of coordinated effort. That operating reality makes us one of the ninety-five people staggering around in search of a finish line.

Ask yourself: Would you rather be one of the five people with a plan . . . or one of the ninety-five people without a plan?

You Do Have to Choose, But . . .

Instead of asking you to make that choice right now, I'm going to ask you to consider how maybe, just maybe, you have been *keeping* yourself from making that choice up to this point.

Is it possible that *you* have been keeping yourself from creating and executing the right plan? Stranger things have happened in life. Fortunately, though, there's a solution to that problem: Read this book and complete the implementation activities at the conclusion of each chapter.

> **Is it possible that *you* have been keeping yourself from creating and executing the right plan? Stranger things have happened in life.**

Once you master the eleven insights you will find in the main section of this book and complete all the activities I will share with you, you will be ready to create a life-plan that makes sense for you, start executing it, and start running toward a clear finish line.

At that point, you really will be in the right place at the right time, no matter where you are, and no matter what time it is.

Shall we get started?

PRINCIPLE

1

»»» There is no growth without pain.

f you've been functioning in your "comfort zone" on a day-to-day basis, feeling rather more or less satisfied with your selling activity and productivity, then it's a good bet that you are producing at a level below your capacity. That's because reaching higher levels of success almost always involves change, which consecutively requires you to venture *out* of your comfort zone.

In order to change and grow—personally or professionally—you will have to modify your behavior and do things a little differently than you have become accustomed to doing them up until now. You will have to alter some preconceived ideas about what is appropriate, how prospects think and act, what people will think of you, and, most important, what you yourself are capable of accomplishing.

As if making those kinds of changes weren't enough, you'll also need to learn to act with confidence and courage at times when you're not feeling particularly confident or courageous. You'll have to develop the discipline to focus on the task at hand when you'd much rather be doing something else. And you'll have to disengage from some reactions and behaviors that have become second nature to you.

Many people will say they are willing to do "whatever it takes" to achieve a goal—until it's actually time to produce.

All of these changes are prerequisites to building dramatic growth in sales—or in any other area of your life.

While growth may not be easy, it is possible. But, it takes a commitment to do what needs to be done *when* it needs to be done. Many people make commitments to getting things done, and then almost immediately make excuses why they can't get to it. I bet you know someone like that.

Many people will say they are willing to do "whatever it takes" to achieve a goal—until it's actually time to produce. Then they start making excuses. "It's too tough," "It'll take too long," and "I didn't

9

realize it was this involved" are common reasons given for backing out of the commitment and abandoning the opportunity to grow.

Have you ever wondered why people give up so quickly on the opportunity to grow? There is an answer.

At the age of five or six, when we were sent off to school to be educated intellectually, we were fairly well programmed emotionally about how to act, and to a great extent, how to think. Our parents taught us what behavior was good and what was bad, what behavior was right and what was wrong, and what behavior was acceptable and what was unacceptable. All of that information served us well when we were small. It provided us with a pattern of behavior to exhibit in situations we were ill equipped to evaluate on our own.

The question is, Can we break free of early childhood programming and exercise our free will to change and grow?

We were taught, for instance, not to talk to strangers; we were taught that "money" matters were not topics for public discussion; perhaps we were taught only to speak when spoken to. We learned these and hundreds of other lessons in our early years. Unfortunately, we were not taught that it would be OK to ignore those childhood admonitions later in our adult life, when the situations were different or we were better able to evaluate our circumstances.

As a result, those patterns of behavior still play in our heads and become the sources of discomfort when we are called on to act in a different manner. Without knowing exactly why, we feel uneasy or uncertain in those situations.

As a child, the discomfort we experienced served as a warning. It protected us when we drifted from the *accepted* behavior—what mom told us to do—and wandered into *dangerous* territory—what mom told us not to do. It caused us to pull back before we got into too much trouble. As an adult, when we experience the same discomfort, the preprogrammed tendency to "pull back" still kicks in. That tendency, along with the uncertain feelings (and the accompanying fears we conjure up), prevents us from wandering too far outside our comfort zone.

So, the question is, Can we break free of early childhood programming and exercise our free will to change and grow?

Pat Makes the Break

Pat works for an information technology consulting firm. He was one of the technical specialists providing support to the salespeople. He had become the primary "go to" person and often accompanied the salespeople on sales calls. He was very comfortable interacting with prospects, asking questions to methodically diagnose their situations and analyze the technical aspects of their requirements.

It was not unusual for Pat to hear, "We couldn't have done it without you" from the salespeople. The words, however, cut like a double-edged sword.

Whether it is modifying programs or configuring networks to meet clients' unique needs, Pat could be counted on to come up with the most innovative and cost-effective solutions. The salespeople were quick to admit that it was Pat's ability to analyze complex situations and develop simple solutions that had enabled them to close sales that otherwise would not have been closed.

It was not unusual for Pat to hear, "We couldn't have done it without you" from the salespeople. The words, however, cut like a double-edged sword. Pat appreciated the praise, but at the same time he was envious, perhaps even resentful, of the large commissions the salespeople earned from *his* expertise.

Recognizing his ability to work well with prospects and customers, both the sales manager and the VP of sales encouraged Pat to "take a stab" at selling. On several occasions, they had offered him the opportunity to develop his own accounts. Each time, he responded with an offhand comment such as, "I oughta give it a try . . . just as soon as things calm down a bit."

You'd think Pat would have jumped at the chance to develop his own accounts. He understood the company's products inside and out. He was effective in communicating with prospects and clients, knowing when to dial back the technical jargon and when to turn it up. And, he had proved, time and time again, his ability to analyze prospects' needs and develop appropriate solutions.

So, why didn't Pat "jump?"

Pat was intrigued by the opportunity to develop his own accounts and the opportunity to earn more money was appealing. But, Pat was hesitant. He felt uneasy moving into sales. He clearly understood that making the leap would take him out of his comfort zone, which was the purely technical aspects of the sale.

Pat had always been brought into the picture *after* the initial contact was made and the need established. Someone else identified and qualified the opportunity before he showed up to "do his magic." He recognized that to develop his own opportunities, he would have to scout them out and qualify them. He would have to make prospecting calls—something he had never done before. He would have to help prospects discover what they were missing by not having the products and services his company provided—again, something he had never done. The questions, How do I do all that? and Can I do that? kept running through his head.

So, why didn't Pat "jump?"

Pat also worried about what would happen if he "failed" in the sales arena. There was prestige attached to being the company's "go-to" technical person. He wondered if he would be giving that up if he made the transition into sales.

Pat's concern about having to learn and apply new skills was normal. His concern about how he would be viewed by his colleagues was normal, too. But, the knot he felt in his stomach every time he thought about making the move to sales was not normal. In fact, it was what was holding him back from taking the leap.

Pat discussed his feelings with the sales manager, Gerry, who was eager to see Pat make the transition. Gerry reassured him that the uneasiness he was feeling was normal and that he would receive all the help necessary to develop his selling skills.

Pat appreciated the encouragement and reassurance. However, he still felt somewhat uncomfortable. He couldn't help but recall something his mother used to say when he was a child: "Don't pretend to be something you're not." Interestingly, he couldn't remember any of the circumstances for which that "advice" was given. Nonetheless, the admonition had stuck for all those years and it was making it difficult for him to leave his comfort zone—his tech world where he was the expert—and take a chance on succeeding in the sales world where he was clearly a novice.

It took about ninety days or so for Pat to develop a rhythm of productive behavior.

Despite the worries, fears, and doubts, Pat eventually took the leap. And, yes, he experienced all the pains, problems, and challenges new salespeople experience. He struggled with prospecting phone calls. Several people cut him off in mid sentence, said they weren't interested, and hung up. Some ended the call with the ubiquitous request for literature. And, others requested that he call back at a later time—which he did—and then they wouldn't take his call.

He muddled his way through initial appointments, attempting to "qualify" the opportunity the way he was taught. Sometimes he came away with the necessary information; sometimes he didn't.

Pat made presentations to people who turned out not to have final buying authority or an appropriate-sized budget. In other words, he made all the mistakes rookie salespeople usually make, but he kept at it, and kept learning.

Despite the discomfort—which he prayed would be "short term" as Gerry continually reminded him during their regular coaching sessions—Pat was committed to "hanging in." He wasn't a quitter.

It took about ninety days or so for Pat to develop a rhythm of productive behavior. His prospecting calls became more polished and more effective. It became much easier asking the hard questions required for qualifying opportunities. His apprehension about asking prospects to make commitments to future actions had also disappeared.

Reflecting on those ninety days, Pat revealed that not a day had gone by that he didn't *quit* the job—at least mentally—or ask himself, What am I doing? His doubts and fears were ever-present at the beginning. But, he was able to put them aside . . . at least long enough to do what needed to be done. Eventually, his doubts and fears faded into the background. Pat wasn't "pretending" to be a salesperson— he *was* a salesperson. And, the commission checks he was now receiving—large commission checks—were proof of that.

In «« «
Summary

Pat knew at the outset that transitioning into sales wasn't going to be easy.

He knew that he would have to go through a period during which he wouldn't have all the answers, he would be uncomfortable, and he would experience failures.

He also had an inner sense that he could—and would—succeed, especially since he had the help and encouragement of his peers.

Pat was willing to endure some short-term pain in exchange for long-term results.

Are you?

Time for
REFLECTION ⟪ ⟪ ⟪
Have You Been "Playing it Safe"?

» Make a list of personal and/or professional "growth" opportunity goals you've been avoiding or have put on hold.

» What have you wanted to be able to do, to know, to be known for, to learn?

» For each goal, identify the benefits—tangible and intangible— that would accrue to you, your family, your business, your community, etc., when you achieve the goal.

» Next, rate your commitment to each goal on a 1-to-5 scale, where 1 represents a weak commitment and 5 represents an undeniable commitment.

» Be brutally honest with your rating. If you've "always wanted to learn to play the piano," for instance, but you've never opened the phone book or checked the Web to locate a music school, the goal likely deserves a rating no greater than 1.

» Focusing on the goals you labeled with a 5, identify the roadblocks—real or imagined—that have held you back.

» What are the "pains" you will have to endure in order to pursue each goal? No excuses allowed—it's a time to be truthful. What, exactly, has prevented you from pursuing the goal? Is it fear of failing or, perhaps, looking foolish? Is it the perceived "hard work" that's put you off? Is it self-doubt or a lack of self-confidence?

» What resources—people, training, education—are available to help you lessen the pain?

» Are you willing to ask for help? Are you willing to accept help?

» Finally, and most importantly, are you willing to do whatever it takes, for however long it takes, to reach your goal? **IMPORTANT: If your answer isn't a resounding "yes," consider the possibility that the goal doesn't actually deserve a commitment rating of 5!**

15

>>> **Keep your belly button covered.**

Selling is an emotional experience shrouded by an intellectual process.

On the surface, selling appears to be a rather intellectual process: matching products and services with people who have a need for those products and services. If there's a match, you make a presentation—demonstrating the goodness of fit—obtain the prospect's commitment, deliver the product or service, and get paid for your efforts. If there's not a match, you move on to someone else.

If it were only that clear-cut . . . and that easy.

First of all, in order to match products and services with people who need them, you must search out and contact those people—people who, for the most part, simply want to go about their day without being interrupted.

Then there are the gatekeepers who do their best to prevent you from actually talking to the person you're trying to reach. Bounce off of enough of them and you might get the sense that their mission in life is to insulate their bosses from the outside world . . . or at least from you.

> On the surface, selling appears to be a rather intellectual process: matching products and services with people who have a need for those products and services.

Finally, in those instances in which you do get through to the decision makers, you find many of them simply don't have the desire or time to engage in a conversation with you. Fifteen seconds into the call, they tell you to "Send me some information about your company. If I'm interested, I'll get back to you," and then they're gone.

Clearly, there *is* an emotional component to this job.

How about the people who *do* talk to you? Many of them don't need or want what you have to sell.

19

And, some—perhaps, many—of the people who need what you have to sell, and to whom you deliver your presentation, don't buy from you. Early in your career, you hear "no" considerably more than you hear "yes."

The selling process, by its very nature, is filled with the opportunity for rejection.

How much rejection must you take?

A lot, if you are to thrive in the world of sales!

While making cold calls is not a "forever" strategy (although seasoned sales professionals still make some cold calls), it is likely a significant part of your early career. That means having to deal with "rejection" is also a significant part of your early career.

You are not a robotic selling machine devoid of feelings. You are human.

If you were a selling automaton, you could go from one prospect to the next, from one potential opportunity to another, paying little or no attention to the rejection. You'd simply be looking for that cold prospect you could turn into a hot prospect and eventually a customer. You would never take the rejection personally. You would never interpret the prospect's rejection of your product or service or the opportunity to discuss it with you as a rejection of *you*. You would never be thinking, "What's wrong with me?" You'd be thinking, "What's wrong with that prospect?"

But, you are not a robotic selling machine devoid of feelings. You are human. And, at some point, experiencing one rejection after another, you begin to think, "Why me?" and "What am I doing wrong?" You begin to interpret the rejection as failure. Not merely failure in a particular selling role—capturing the prospect's attention or connecting your product or service to the prospect's needs, for instance—but personal failure . . . failure as an individual!

Where did that attitude and its accompanying feelings come from? Many salespeople blame the prospects.

Ed Takes It Personally

Ed represents a process engineering consulting firm. He was calling on manufacturing companies that responded to an ad in a trade journal. His first call was on Clarkson Manufacturing. He walked in, introduced himself to the receptionist, and asked to speak to Bill Deavers, the CEO. As she picked up the phone and punched the buttons, she pointed to a row of chairs and told Ed to have a seat.

A few minutes later, Mr. Deavers entered the reception area, walked over to Ed and said, "I'm Bill Deavers. What do you want?" Ed responded, "Thanks for seeing me, Mr. Deavers. I'm Ed Lucas with Pro Max Associates. We've been very successful in helping manufacturing companies like yours improve manufacturing throughput an average of 23 percent while keeping reject rates under one-half of 1 percent. You had requested . . ."

Now, after a sixty-second encounter with a stranger, he felt like a peddler who went door to door begging for an opportunity to sell his wares.

"Hold it," Mr. Deavers interrupted. "I was in the middle of a meeting. I don't have time for this nonsense." He then turned his back to Ed, walked over to the receptionist, and asked if the mail had been delivered. She handed him a pile of envelopes that he began sorting through.

"Nonsense." The word resonated in Ed's mind. Ed walked over to the reception desk, not sure what to say or whether to say anything at all. He finally got up the courage to blurt out, "Excuse me." The receptionist turned toward him, but Mr. Deavers continued to sort through the envelopes, ignoring Ed's presence. Ed stood there for what seemed like several minutes, but was actually about fifteen seconds, then turned and walked out.

Five minutes later, Ed was in a coffee shop, sipping a cup of his favorite coffee blend—Sumatra Extra Bold. If only Ed himself were feeling "extra bold," but he wasn't. He was feeling terrible. Mr. Deavers' words, "I don't have time for this nonsense" and the picture of him standing with his back to Ed, ignoring him, kept playing over and over in his mind. He had started the day feeling optimistic and enthusiastic. But now, after a sixty-second encounter with a stranger, he felt like a peddler who went door to door begging for an opportunity to sell his wares.

Ed took the rejection *personally.* He was feeling dejected and de-motivated, looking for any reason to abandon the prospecting and return to the office. All of this was because of a brief encounter with a prospect who didn't have the decency to extend a little common courtesy.

> **Neither Mr. Deavers nor the prospects and gatekeepers you will encounter—nor anyone else, for that matter—has a magic umbilical cord they can plug in to your belly button.**

An intellectual assessment of the situation might allow us to surmise that Mr. Deavers was having a bad day *before* Ed showed up, not *because* Ed showed up. Perhaps the meeting he was engaged in was going poorly and Ed was a convenient person on whom to unload his frustration. Ed had nothing to do with Mr. Deavers' behavior. He should have ignored it and moved on to his next call.

Beyond the Emotional Reaction

Ed's reaction is typical of many salespeople. It was strictly *emotional.* What's worse, rather than owning his feelings, which would have allowed him to deal with them, he rationalized (and devalued) them by blaming Mr. Deavers for the way he felt.

In Ed's mind, if Mr. Deavers hadn't treated him so poorly, by ignoring him and characterizing the reason for his visit as "nonsense," Ed himself wouldn't be feeling the way he did. It's as if Mr. Deavers figuratively plugged in a magic umbilical cord into Ed's belly button and drained Ed of his confidence, courage, drive, persistence, and self-esteem—all the positive feelings he possessed before the encounter—leaving him with feelings of fear, worry, and doubt.

Neither Mr. Deavers nor the prospects and gatekeepers you will encounter—nor anyone else, for that matter—has a magic umbilical cord they can plug in to your belly button. They can't transfer feelings in either direction. They can't make you feel one way or another.

> **If you've been blaming others for the way you feel, stop! Cover up your belly button. Don't allow anyone to plug in.**

Your feelings are the result of *your* thinking, your interpretations of events. Moreover, you are free to interpret events any way you want. You can give them a positive spin and create positive feelings, or you can give them a negative spin and create negative feelings. The choice is yours—not the prospect's, not the gatekeeper's, not anyone else's.

If you've been blaming others for the way you feel, stop! Cover up your belly button. Don't allow anyone to plug in.

After losing an "arm wrestling match" with a receptionist, for instance, you might think of *yourself* as a loser—someone who can't even get past a gatekeeper and have a call put through to a decision maker. If you take that view, you allow the gatekeeper to symbolically "plug in" and siphon away some of your self-esteem.

You Can Learn to Look at the Event Differently

You can view the prospect company as the loser. As a result of the gatekeeper's misguided mission, the company lost the opportunity— at least for the time being—to benefit from your product or service.

You can look at the temporary setback as a learning experience— an example of what not to repeat in the future. And, you can view it as a challenge—an opportunity to develop a more innovative way to get to the decision maker. In other words, you can choose to find positive outcomes from negative experiences. No one else can make that choice for you. It is yours and yours alone. The feelings attached to those outcomes are also yours and yours alone. They were not transferred from or altered by anyone else.

There is only one person responsible for your feelings: you!

In «««
Summary

The sales arena is an environment filled with emotions from both ends of the spectrum.

There are the highs of closing the big sale you've been working on for months, the lows of watching similar opportunities awarded to your competition, and everything in between.

You will encounter people who appreciate your efforts and complement you.

You'll also encounter people who will have little regard for or appreciation of your efforts.

How you interpret these events—the feelings you associate with the experiences—is entirely up to you.

You can choose to associate positive feelings or negative feelings with a given prospect or customer.

Only you can decide. No one else can make that choice for you.

Time for
REFLECTION ‹‹ ‹‹ ‹‹

Do You Own Your Feelings?

Interactions with customers, colleagues, friends, family, and strangers take many different shapes. Some are warm, friendly, and comforting. Others are quite different. They are cold, calculating, and confrontational. Similarly, the feelings we experience from these interactions are just as varied and run the gamut from mad and sad at one end of the spectrum to happy and excited at the other end. Regardless of what you are feeling or why, the feelings are yours and yours alone. You *choose* to generate them. And, at the time, they serve a purpose. They direct or provide justification for a particular course of action, but not necessarily for the most appropriate or positive course of action.

» Identify situations in which your feelings serve little or no positive purpose.

  » Feeling (and, perhaps, expressing) anger and walking away because a prospect didn't buy your product or service or because your son didn't make the basketball team are two examples.

» Identify the real "purpose" those feeling serve.

  » What do they protect?

  » Do they enable you to avoid facing real issues?

  » What other feelings do they mask?

» For each situation, identify an alternative feeling that would serve a more positive purpose. Describe the feeling and the purpose.

  » For example, feeling and showing empathy, rather than anger, if your son didn't make the basketball team is probably a more effective way of helping him deal with his disappointment.

>>>> No one can enter your castle
without your permission.

Only you have the key to your castle.

The selling process, as you have discovered, is filled with the opportunity for rejection. If that weren't enough, frustration and disappointment are also part of the landscape.

It's inescapable.

There will be prospects who definitely need what you have to sell, but who won't recognize it regardless of what you tell them, show them, or help them experience.

There will also be those who recognize the need, but who will refuse to admit that it applies to them or their company. "Others in our industry, but not us," they will say.

And finally, there will be those who recognize and acknowledge the need, but who will put off taking any action for reasons that no one can explain.

What goes on in the outer world cannot affect you because you are safe and secure in your castle.

Each and every day you venture into the sales arena, you will inevitably set yourself up to experience rejection, frustration, and disappointment. How will you prevent this "hostile" environment from having a detrimental impact on your inner core—your psychological well-being? In the preceding chapters, we discussed not allowing others to "plug in" and we discussed taking responsibility for your feelings. However, there is more to it than that.

Understand that your inner world—your psychological makeup and your sense of self—is different than your outer world, which, in this case, is the role you play in the sales arena.

Imagine your inner world existing within an elaborate castle. A castle with huge, impenetrable doors—to which only you have the key—surrounded by an enormous moat filled with ferocious creatures. In your castle, you are secure. With the doors securely locked and the drawbridge that crosses the moat lifted high, your self-worth and your intrinsic value as a human being are protected from outside influences. What goes on in the outer world cannot affect you because you are safe and secure in your castle.

> ## No one can enter your castle and harm you or devalue your self-worth. The events of the outer world remain in the outer world.

Each day, you don your suit of armor—your confidence, courage, and high self-esteem—unlock the castle doors, lower the bridge across the moat, and venture off into the outer world—the sales arena. Some encounters will be nonthreatening and rewarding. There will, however, be times when you experience rejection, frustration, and disappointment. While those experiences may temporarily dent your armor, at any time during the day you can retreat across the drawbridge into your castle, raise the bridge, lock the doors, and once again be safe and secure, with your self-worth intact. No one can enter your castle and harm you or devalue your self-worth. The events of the outer world remain in the outer world.

"Outer world experiences cannot affect my inner world." What if you actually lived by that credo? Regardless of how many dents and dings your armor endures—stalls, put-offs, or objections, gatekeepers and prospects that turn you away, and prospects who enthusiastically view your presentations and then say "no"—when you return to your castle, your self-worth would still be intact.

On any given day, your sales performance might have been lacking (in fact, it may have been horrible), and your armor was severely dented, but your self-worth—your value as an individual—would not be diminished one bit because it was safe and protected in your castle.

Linda the Warrior

Linda was the business development director for a management consulting firm. Part of her responsibility was to identify prospective clients and schedule appointments for the account executives. She spent half of her time on the phone prospecting—making cold calls, following up on referrals, and responding to marketing and advertising leads.

The CEO depended on Linda to find quality prospects. The account execs depended on her to keep them busy with appointments. You might think that she was under a lot of pressure. But, Linda didn't feel pressure. She actually enjoyed prospecting. It was a game of sorts—a challenge to see how many prospects' defenses she could penetrate. She knew that prospects would "fight" back, but she was prepared.

> **Separating your inner world from your outer world doesn't relieve you of the responsibility of developing the skills and committing to the behavior necessary to make the most of your outer-world experience.**

Before Linda left the security of her castle—in this case, her other job responsibilities—lowered the bridge, and crossed the moat to "do battle" with prospects, she put on her symbolic suit of armor. It consisted of a tan western-style leather vest and a dark brown beret. The *armor* allowed her to leave the secure role of business development *director* and step into the role of business development *warrior*, knowing she would be safe. Her armor, though it made a dubious fashion statement, protected her from the comments of stubborn gatekeepers or discourteous prospects.

When she finished "doing battle," she would return to her castle, take off her armor, and return to her other duties unscathed. The ritual of putting on her "armor" served to separate her two worlds and enabled her to ease into the required mind-set to be effective in her prospecting pursuits.

However, separating your inner world from your outer world doesn't relieve you of the responsibility of developing the skills and committing to the behavior necessary to make the most of your outer-world experience. Leaving your outer world in shambles each day as you retreat to your castle is not a strategy for reaching high levels of success. Separating the two worlds does, however, allow you to look back at the outer world with a clear perspective. From the safety of your castle, you can review and analyze what took place from an objective point of view. You can make an intellectual, rather than emotional, analysis of your performance and decide which skills need to be improved and which strategies need to be adjusted for your next excursion into the outer world.

In «««
Summary

Your experiences in the outer world are just that: *outer world* experiences, and that's where they must remain.

When you cross the bridge to re-enter your castle, you must leave those experiences behind.

In the outer world, you will have winning and losing experiences. In your castle—your inner world—you will always be a winner.

In your castle, your self-worth will always be high, regardless of what occurred in the outer world.

Time for
REFLECTION ⫷ ⫷ ⫷

Is Your Castle Secure?

Are you allowing unpleasant experiences to linger on in your thoughts long after the event has ended?

» Identify situations in which you can't seem to "let go," and in which holding on to the thoughts and feelings surrounding the events adversely impacts your self-esteem.

» Example: Continuing to think about, talk about, and feel bad about an instance in which a prospect was critical of your sales efforts.

» For each occurrence, identify why you simply can't let go and what purpose, if any, is being served by doing so.

» Identify how you must alter your actions and thought processes to be able to leave the thoughts and feelings about the experiences in the outer world.

» If, for instance, there is a lesson to be learned from the experience, can it be learned quickly rather than by continually rehashing the incident?

PRINCIPLE
4

≫ ≫ ≫ **Avoid reach-back and after-burn.**

Worry is interest paid in advance on borrowed trouble.

In the previous chapter, you learned that your castle can provide you with a safe haven—a place to regroup, to review your performance with an impartial eye, and to objectively prepare for your next challenge. But, that is only true if you actually leave your outer world in the outer world. If you carry some of those outer-world experiences— past, present, or future—and the feelings and attitudes attached to those experiences back across the bridge into your castle, you can pollute your inner world.

This pollution usually manifests in the form of worry either about a future event, known as *reach-back*, or about a previous event, known as *after-burn*. Reach-back is the situation in which thoughts about a future event "reach back" and have a negative impact on your current behavior. After-burn is the flip side of the worry coin. It is the situation in which thoughts about a past event are carried forward and have a negative impact on your current behavior.

> **If you carry some of those outer-world experiences—past, present, or future— and the feelings and attitudes attached to those experiences back across the bridge into your castle, you can pollute your inner world.**

Tim Pays Interest

Tim is the project leader for an engineering firm. He had an important presentation on Monday afternoon. He scheduled enough time on the preceding Friday to carefully plan his presentation and then rehearse it several times. He prepared answers to the questions he anticipated his prospect would ask. He double-checked his visuals and triple-checked his talking points. He was confident that all bases were covered.

Despite the fact that Tim set aside additional time on Monday morning to give the presentation a final review and run-through, he carted all the presentation material home on Friday. He planned to invest a little time that evening giving the material one last visual check while his wife and kids were out shopping. Tim spent about two hours reviewing his material and rehearsing his presentation. He was so thoroughly prepared that he could practically deliver the presentation in his sleep. That should have been the end of it.

It wasn't.

Saturday, a day usually reserved for family activities, Tim found himself "mentally living" the Monday presentation over and over again. Sunday morning, Tim gave up his golf game to run through his presentation one more time and make sure he hadn't missed anything during his Friday-evening preparations. Several times during the day on Sunday, he found himself thinking about his upcoming presentation, worrying that he had overlooked some critical element.

> **Worry is not a healthy emotion. Worrying is not a constructive activity. It clouds your thinking and diverts your attention from real issues to imagined scenarios that rarely develop and over which you have little or no control.**

The time Tim spent on Friday planning and preparing for his presentation was appropriate and an intelligent investment of his time. But the time he spent over the weekend worrying about the presentation was unproductive and unnecessary. He allowed his fears and concerns about a two-hour future event to reach back and consume his weekend. Tim was paying interest in advance on borrowed trouble.

Worry is not a healthy emotion. Worrying is not a constructive activity. It clouds your thinking and diverts your attention from real issues to imagined scenarios that rarely develop and over which you have little or no control. It obscures your judgment and prevents logical, objective analysis. In short, worry—especially reach-back-induced worry—serves no value.

Tim delivered his presentation on Monday afternoon as scheduled. He covered each point of his proposal and provided comprehensive answers to each of the buying committee members' questions. They were impressed with the thoroughness of his presentation and very comfortable with his answers to their questions.

> **An intelligent assessment of his presentation, perhaps a fifteen- or twenty-minute debrief with his sales manager, would have been appropriate.**

While the buying committee wasn't making the final buying decision, they were whittling down the number of proposals for consideration and a final decision by the CEO. At the end of the presentation, Joe, the committee leader, told Tim that his proposal would be one of the three submitted to the CEO, and Tim would be informed of the final decision on Friday. Joe wished Tim "good luck." Then, as he shook Tim's hand, he revealed, "If the decision were up to me, you would get the contract."

Driving back to the office, Tim kept replaying Joe's words in his mind. He was getting mixed signals. Was Joe being supportive or was he sending another, less positive, message? Tim couldn't help but wonder if there wasn't an unspoken "but . . ." following Joe's words. For instance: "If the decision were up to me, you would get the contract, *but I think the CEO is leaning toward a different approach.*"

Tim spent the balance of the day sitting at his desk replaying Joe's comment in his mind. He tried to recall the inflection of the words—anything that might reveal their true intent. The more he thought about it, the more concerned he became.

Tim began to worry.

Tuesday morning, Tim shared his concerns with a colleague, who told him, "Let it go. What's done is done. There's nothing you can do now, anyway." Tim knew that was good advice, but he couldn't "let it go."

Joe's words continued to haunt him. For the next two days, Tim replayed in his mind his interactions with the prospect account from the very first contact. His worry turned to self-doubt: What did I miss? Where did I go off track? What should I have done differently?

Tim had not prepared intellectually or emotionally for "what if" situations.

An intelligent assessment of his presentation, perhaps a fifteen- or twenty-minute debrief with his sales manager, would have been appropriate. But, spending several days in a cloud of worry, fear, and self-doubt was unnecessary and unproductive. Replaying Monday's presentation over and over all week prevented Tim from focusing on current activities and getting anything else accomplished, which created additional problems. Tim was not only worrying about the outcome of his presentation, but he was beginning to feel guilty about his lack of attention to other activities. Worry, doubts, feelings of guilt: Tim was definitely caught in a downward spiral heading straight for depression.

How did that happen?

When Tim began developing his presentation, his primary concern was to cross all the t's, dot all the i's, and convincingly connect the features and advantages of his company's services to the specific needs of the prospect. All of his preparation and rehearsal was focused on "getting it right."

Tim never considered, "What if . . ."

≫ my presentation is off track?

≫ I missed some critical information?

≫ I can't answer all of the committee members' questions?

Tim had not prepared intellectually or emotionally for "what if" situations. He never gave a moment's thought to the possibility that his initial analysis of the prospective client's situation might have been inaccurate or that his presentation might miss the mark. Consequently, the specter of "failure"—the worst-case interpretation of Joe's comment—paralyzed him. Tim had allowed himself to become a victim of after-burn.

Beating Reach-Back and After-Burn

Both reach-back and after-burn are emotionally driven processes fueled by fears, worries, and doubts. The remedy for avoiding them, however, is intellectually driven.

Reach-back can be avoided with intelligent organization. Designate a specific amount of time for planning and preparation for future events. Then, schedule the time so it doesn't interfere with other normal activities. Finally, and most importantly, give yourself permission to keep to the schedule, and then *let it go!* Overindulging in preparation—like overindulging in chocolate or alcohol—may make you feel good for a while, but there will be a price to pay, and it won't be pleasant.

> Reach-back **can be avoided with intelligent organization. Designate a specific amount of time for** planning and preparation **for future events.**

After-burn can be avoided by accepting the possibility of a less-than-perfect outcome. Sometimes, your undertakings will be carried out flawlessly, exactly as planned, and you'll achieve your desired result. That's good. Other times, you'll stumble and fall and fail to achieve your goal. That's not so good, but it's part of the human experience. *Accept it!* The world will continue to rotate on its axis and revolve around the sun, and you'll survive to live another day and fight another battle.

To minimize the effects of after-burn, recognize that experiencing a less-than-optimum outcome can be beneficial. In every "failing" experience, there is an opportunity to learn, to extract a lesson that will prevent future failures. You pay the price once and reap the benefits forever. Once you've identified the lesson, you can turn your attention away from the event from which you obtained it (ending the after-burn), and focus on future situations to which you can apply it.

After-burn can be avoided by accepting the possibility of a less-than-perfect outcome.

You can further minimize reach-back and after-burn by thoughtfully planning your week and then prioritizing and organizing your daily activities. If today's activities are well organized, you should be able to start tomorrow's activities without after-burn. And, if tomorrow's activities are thoughtfully planned, you should be able to complete today's activities without reach-back.

In «««
Summary

Worrying about an event that has yet to occur or one that has previously occurred is like worrying about the weather.

No matter how deep or profound your concerns are, they won't change anything.

Time for
REFLECTION
Are You Wasting Energy?

Worry is not a substitute for proper planning and review. Focus your energy on action, not worry.

» Identify two events—one personal and one professional—you tend to worry about in advance.

» For each of those events, identify your concerns or the aspects of the events on which your worry is focused.

» Describe the action steps you can take to better plan for those aspects and concerns and thereby eliminate the need for worry.

» In the same way, identify two events you tend to worry about after the fact.

» For each of those events, identify the aspects of the event on which your after-the-fact worry is focused.

» Describe the action steps you can take prior to and/or during the event to eliminate the need to worry after the fact.

5

>>>> There's a difference between
who you "I" and what you "R."

You can only perform in your roles in a manner consistent with how you see yourself conceptually.

Early in his selling career, David Sandler was struck by how differently people responded to his sales efforts. Some prospects were extremely cordial, some were merely accommodating, and others were out-and-out rude. Sandler set out to discover what drives people to act so differently. In his quest, he discovered Transactional Analysis (TA). TA provided the answer he was looking for.

Sandler learned enough from TA to value the psychology of human dynamics in professional selling. It seemed that no one had previously made the connection. The human-relations model of TA provided the foundation on which he developed the Sandler Selling System. (We'll explore TA in the next chapter.)

> ## Sandler discovered that many people related their self-worth (self-identity, self-esteem, self-image, or simply *identity*) to their role performance.

Sandler observed that success for some people came almost effortlessly, while others with the same training, selling the same products and services in the same market, struggled for every victory and rarely reached the highest levels of success. Determined to find out the difference between the two groups, Sandler became a student of human behavior. His research led him to the discovery of the interconnected nature of an individual's role performance and self-identity.

Sandler discovered that many people related their self-worth (self-identity, self-esteem, self-image, or simply *identity*) to their role performance. If they performed particularly well in a role, they felt good about themselves and felt as though they were worth more. If they didn't do well, they didn't feel good about themselves and felt like they were worth less—not just as a role performer, but as a human being.

For these people, self-worth was being shaped by their successes and failures in their various roles. Over time, they developed a self-worth image ranging from very low to very high.

Why did they make that connection?

Roles

When you were born, you had no conscious roles; you were yourself. As you grew up, your parents and others began to assign to you various roles—daughter or son, brother or sister, student, friend, playmate. You have continued to acquire roles throughout your life as you have formed new relationships, such as marriage, and tried new activities at work and in your leisure time.

Every role has "rules" or expectations that define what constitutes good performance in that role. Good children obey their parents. Good students get high grades. Good salespeople close big sales.

Most of the time, you'll find that the praise and rewards you receive are connected to your role performance. The same is true of the criticism and penalties. When you cleaned your room, your mom rewarded you with a hug and perhaps a cookie. You earned her acceptance, not simply for being you, but instead for completing the task of cleaning your room.

> **Most of the time, you'll find that the praise and rewards you receive are connected to your role performance.**

When you received good grades, your parents praised you and colleges offered you scholarships. Your teacher probably didn't report to your parents that, in addition to having an aptitude for math, you had a healthy sense of your own worth. When you hit a winning home run in a softball game, your friends and teammates commented on it for days afterward. They probably never complimented you for just being yourself.

When you exceeded your sales goal several months in a row, you got a large bonus. There weren't any rewards during the months when you remained self-confident despite some setbacks.

This type of feedback—from parents, teachers, bosses, etc.—is how you came to believe that your worth depended on how well you performed your roles.

If you confuse your role performance with your value as a human being, your self-image will inevitably suffer. After all, you won't excel at everything you try to do. No one does! The sales arena, as you've discovered in earlier chapters, is filled with opportunities to experience rejection, frustration, and disappointment. So there's simply no way you can put in a winning performance *all the time.*

Winners, At-Leasters, Losers

The salespeople who achieved consistently high levels of success, Sandler discovered, had high levels of self-esteem regardless of the outcome of any particular sales challenge. They didn't let less-than-excellent performances pollute their Identity.

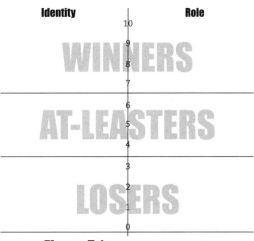

Figure 5.1: I/R Theory Scale

Expanding Dr. Eric Berne's Script Theory, Sandler created a psychological model, called **I/R Theory**, to differentiate between *identity* and *roles* and to help salespeople understand the interconnected nature of these two concepts. He used the accompanying graphic to illustrate the theory (see Figure 5.1).

The left side of the illustration represents the individual's Identity rating on a scale of 0 to 10, with 0 representing a very low level of self-esteem and 10 representing a very high level of self-esteem. The right side of the illustration represents the individual's **R**ole-performance rating on the 0-to-10 scale, with 0 representing poor performance and 10 representing excellent performance.

The I/R Theory describes three psychological positions: Winners, At-Leasters, and Losers. The labels are not judgmental terms, but rather psychological terms with specific meanings.

> **Winners are willing to take risks and try something new or do things differently. They recognize that the outcome of such activities is just that—an outcome—and nothing more.**

Winners are people who consistently rate their Identity between 7 and 10. That is, they have high self-esteem and feel good about themselves regardless of the outcome of their role experiences. They don't need role success to validate their self-worth and they don't allow role failure to devalue their self-worth. Their self-esteem comes from within. Winners are willing to take risks and try something new or do things differently. They recognize that the outcome of such activities is just that—an outcome—and nothing more. Sometimes the outcome will be favorable; sometimes, it won't. In both cases, they accept responsibility. And, neither case will affect their Identity rating.

At the other end of the scale are the Losers. They consistently rate their Identity somewhere between 0 and 3. Losers have low self-esteem. They tend to have little confidence in their abilities and judgment. They don't expect to win and, most often, they don't. Losers are unlikely to try something new or do things differently. After all, if they try something new and don't obtain favorable results, it will only reinforce the poor image they already hold of themselves. And, when Losers do experience role failure, they look for excuses on which to blame the poor result. If they fail to close a sale, for instance, they might blame the economy, the competition, or even their company's pricing policy. Not accepting responsibility extends to positive outcomes as well. If a Loser closes a big or particularly difficult sale, he or she will attribute it to luck. Losers tend to feel victimized by both good and bad luck. They will often resent others for whom success appears to come more easily.

Between the Winners and the Losers are the At-Leasters. Their Identity rating is between 4 and 6. They may not be Winners, but *at least* they are not Losers. Their Identity rating is closely tied to their role performance. Because they don't see themselves as Winners, they don't stretch outside their comfort zone and strive for greater levels of success. At the same time, they don't want to be labeled a Loser or a wimp, so they will do whatever is necessary to maintain the status quo. Sometimes, they make progress and feel good about themselves; sometimes they lose ground and do not feel good about themselves. Over the long run, however, they are Mr. or Ms. Average.

Whatever your psychological position, you will find that you are as successful in your roles as your self-image allows you to be. You will perform in a way that is consistent with the value you place on yourself. This is the result of the tendency we all have to maintain an integration of our R-level with our I-level in order to act in ways that are consistent with how we feel about ourselves.

Michael, the At-Leaster

Michael sells materials-handling equipment—everything from hand trucks and hoists to motorized conveyors and forklifts. He began his seventeen-year career with the company handling stock in the warehouse during the summers

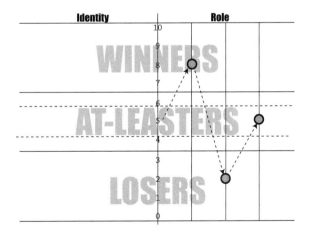

Figure 5.2: Michael's Role Performance

when he was in college. After college, he was offered a position in the company's marketing department. After a few years, Michael worked his way into the sales department, viewing it as a pathway to greater financial reward.

Michael knows as much about the industry, the marketplace, and materials-handling equipment as anyone in the company—more than most, in fact. His knowledge and expertise, one might guess, would guarantee him high levels of success in the sales arena. You would expect him to be the company's top salesperson.

He isn't.

Michael consistently turns in a performance somewhere in the middle of the pack. He is a textbook At-Leaster. On the 0-to-10 scale, his Identity rating is a solid 5. Michael has spent much of his life adjusting his role performance to how he feels about himself.

Michael is caught in his comfort zone.

The need to remain in an At-Leaster or Loser comfort zone can keep you from attaining and maintaining the level of success of which you are capable.

Here is a prime example (see Figure 5.2). During the first month of the quarter, Michael puts in an exceptional performance: He closes eight out of ten opportunities. There can be no doubt that, in his role as a salesperson, Michael is performing at R-8. The problem is that Michael doesn't think of himself as an 8. "I'm good," he may tell himself, "but I'm not that good." With that in mind, he promptly finds a way to adjust his performance. Over the next month, he does some things that will bring his performance down and he closes only two out of ten opportunities. Michael ponders his R-2 performance and thinks, "I'm not great, but I'm not that bad." Over the next month, he adjusts. When he's back selling at an R-5 level, he relaxes again. Michael adjusted his performance in order to bring it back to a level where he was comfortable with it.

Your comfort zone encompasses the values just below and just above the value you place on your I-side. So if you, like Michael, rate your "I" as a 5, your comfort zone will range from I-4 to I-6. To hold that position, you also have to keep your performance between R-4 and R-6. Your self-image defines the limits of your comfort zone and forms the basis of a self-fulfilling prophecy, for better . . . or worse.

The need to remain in an At-Leaster or Loser comfort zone can keep you from attaining and maintaining the level of success of which you are capable. The need for your comfort zone also creates a strong fear of failure, which stops you from taking risks that can open up new options and activities to you. You play it safe and protect your I-side with low-risk selling situations to avoid failing at a high-risk endeavor and reaching higher levels of success.

Where Is the Roadblock?

Anna was twenty-eight years old when she obtained a sales position with a commercial cleaning services company. In her first year with the company, she inherited a (supposedly) abysmal sales territory. The last salesperson who had tried to sell there had failed to meet quota, had been placed on formal notice, and had eventually been let go. At the end of her first year, however, Anna had remarkably earned just over $50,000 in commissions from that supposedly "terrible" territory. Her sales manager, figuring that she would do even better in a more lucrative territory, assigned her a larger territory that had consistently generated between $90,000 and $95,000 in commissions for the former salesperson who had recently retired.

> **Anna had drive and enthusiasm for her work and she exhibited the confidence and competence of a more seasoned professional. So, what was the problem?**

The next year, something unexpected happened. Anna earned $54,300 from that $90,000+ territory—barely 8 percent more than she earned the previous year in a territory with significantly less potential. It was a big disappointment to the sales manager. He thought that perhaps he had moved her up too quickly to a territory that was too large. So, he reassigned her to a somewhat smaller territory where she would be less likely to feel overwhelmed, and in which, by his calculations, she should be able to earn about $70,000 in commissions.

In her third full year of selling for the company, Anna earned $52,700 from that easier-to-manage territory—a bit more than she earned her first year, but a bit less than she earned the previous year. The sales manager began to suspect that the problem wasn't with the territory—it was with Anna. But he couldn't put his finger on what was holding her back. Anna had drive and enthusiasm for her work and she exhibited the confidence and competence of a more seasoned professional. So, what was the problem?

Anna, like Michael, was stuck in her comfort zone, but for a different reason. Anna had a healthy self-image. Unlike Michael, who didn't see himself as a Winner, Anna did see herself as a Winner. But, her benchmark for winning was very different than the benchmark set by her sales manager. You might say Anna was a winner on a 0-to-5 scale.

> **The real roadblock was the deeply imbedded notion that greater levels of success—performing at a higher level on her R-side—*would somehow harm her relationship with her family*, which, in turn, would devalue her self-image.**

Anna grew up in a rural community where her parents and two brothers, with whom she is very close, still reside. The business environment there consists primarily of agriculture, mining, and manufacturing. By hometown standards, a $50,000 income was a sign of "success." Her father, now retired for several years, never earned more than $50,000 per year. And, neither of her brothers, both older than Anna and supporting families, is earning much more than $50,000.

Somewhere in her psyche, Anna held the belief that earning more than $50,000 was somehow "wrong" and attaining any greater level of success—measured, to some extent, by income as well as by the material things it would allow her to obtain—would likely be viewed by her family in an unfavorable light. Perhaps she thought it would send the message that she was better than they are and damage the relationship. Regardless, earning more money would make her uncomfortable.

It was not Anna's current self-image that held her back, as in Michael's case. The real roadblock was the deeply imbedded notion that greater levels of success—performing at a higher level on her R-side—*would somehow harm her relationship with her family*, which, in turn, would devalue her self-image. Anna didn't have a fear of success; she had a fear of *greater* success, based on a standard that wasn't necessarily appropriate for her current situation.

> **Right now, your** comfort zone **is squelching your spirit and confining your** potential**.**

Interestingly, Anna's R-performance when interacting with prospects was consistently between 8 and 10, unlike Michael's, which varied widely. What accounted for her less-than-8-to-10 results, however, was the *inconsistency* of her R-side behavior. Anna was working at a pace that would allow her to keep her level of success in a "safe" zone. Safe, that is, in relation to her preconceived ideas about how to maintain her close family relationship (and not devalue her "I").

Get Out of the Comfort Zone!

If you are a Loser or an At-Leaster, your comfort zone is a comfortable trap from which you need to escape. You may not have thought of your performance in those terms. You may have convinced yourself that you are, in fact, *uncomfortable* with your current level of performance. But the truth of the matter is, you are not yet uncomfortable *enough* with it to change it. That means there's a level of comfort, or—if you prefer—familiarity, to what you are creating in your life right now.

Right now, your comfort zone is squelching your spirit and confining your potential. The good news—and the bad news—is that breaking out is entirely up to you. It is your attitude about yourself that puts you in that restricted place, and it will be your new attitude that gets you out. Instead of adjusting your performance, adjust your sense of self-worth.

When you entered this world, before anyone assigned you roles or imprinted their values and judgments on you, you were an I-10. And, when you leave this world, you will be an I-10. How you value yourself in between those two events is entirely up to you.

Give yourself the I-10 that you deserve.

In «««
Summary

Your self-confidence is as much of an influence, if not a greater one, on your overall success than your skill to perform any task.

Ultimately, your success has more to do with your willingness to "take the leap" to become an I-10 than it does with an intellectual assessment of your abilities or of the ramifications of failure.

Time for
REFLECTION ⟪ ⟪ ⟪
Raising Your Comfort Zone

Take the first step today.

>> Briefly describe a role activity—personal or professional—that you have been avoiding or putting off because of existing or potential I-side discomfort.

>> It might be an activity you continually avoid, such as prospecting, or it might be an activity that involves facing an uncomfortable issue with a friend or relative.

>> Write a brief statement describing the benefit, value, or reward of carrying out the activity you described above. This would be the best-case scenario.

>> Write a brief statement describing consequences of attempting the task or activity and not obtaining the desired result. This would be the worst-case scenario.

>> Describe the I-side risks of attempting the activity or task.

>> Some examples are not knowing what to say or do, being wrong, being embarrassed, discovering the truth, and so on.

>> If the best-case scenario is desirable and the worst-case scenario doesn't lead to a devastating or harmful situation, describe what is needed to commit to and complete the task or activity. It may take nothing more than a word of encouragement from a friend or colleague.

When you have spent a lifetime judging yourself based on your performance, the change in attitude won't happen overnight and will elude you from time to time. You will fall back into old ways of thinking and rationalizing, especially when you are under stress. Should that happen, simply recognize what has taken place and begin working to get back on track.

6

≫≫≫ **People make buying decisions emotionally and justify those decisions intellectually.**

avid Sandler was the first person to formulate as a selling principle the basic idea that people make buying decisions emotionally and justify them intellectually. Sandler was the first to apply this concept to the imperative of identifying the "pain" in a prospect's world. Pain, after all, is a powerful generator of emotion. People have been repeating what he said for years, often without understanding the core concept behind his observation.

What basic human dynamic was Sandler talking about? Let's find out.

Pain, after all, is a powerful generator of emotion.

Why Did He Buy the Boxster?

Brett, a successful real-estate developer, wanted to buy a new car. After doing a little shopping, he settled on a ruby-red metallic Porsche Boxster. The final price of the automobile was $46,000.

When Brett explained the reasons behind the purchase to his wife, Eleanor, he emphasized the following: the dealer gave him a $2,400 discount off the $48,400 sticker price; there was no charge for scheduled maintenance for four years; the dealer was offering 0.9 percent financing; the car has the most advanced electronic stability control system in its class; and *Car and Driver* spoke glowingly about the automobile's elegant design and performance.

When he was relaxing with his buddies, however, Brett gave a very different reason for purchasing the car: "The minute I got behind the wheel," he told them over a beer, "I felt like a kid again, like a teenager getting his first car."

Emotional Motivation

This story illustrates what Sandler was telling us—that *important human decisions inevitably arise from emotions*. Brett's decision to purchase the Porsche did not start when he learned about the electronic stability control system, or when he tracked down the *Car and Driver* article, or when he negotiated the $2,400 discount, or when he found out about the no-charge scheduled maintenance. All of that happened *after* the event that really triggered the sale: Brett sat down behind the wheel of the sports car and felt free. He even told his friends that he "felt like a kid again," and those words were truer, perhaps, than he realized. The **emotional motivation** is what drove the decision process, and that emotional motivation, as we'll see in just a moment, had a great deal to do with Brett's feeling "like a kid again."

> **The decision to take action on something will *always* emerge from the realm of emotion first, and will typically connect to a pain we are trying to avoid or a pleasure we are eager to experience.**

Here are some questions: Suppose Brett's stock portfolio had collapsed the day before he was to finalize the paperwork with the dealer? Suppose he had lost his job the day before, and suddenly found himself facing a new and uncertain world, a world without any prospects of future income? Suppose his wife had gotten wind of the proposed purchase beforehand and promised to divorce him if he signed off on the deal? In these situations, and in any number of others, Brett's initial impulse to buy would have been effectively vetoed by other "voices" within his mind. He still would have had the freedom to choose which voice to follow, of course, but the voice that said "I feel like a kid again" would have come from a very different place than the voice that said to him, "This is not the right move to make, given the current circumstances."

What are these voices, and where do they come from? Once we know the answer to this question, we can begin to understand this critical success principle.

No Emotion, No Decision

If a prospect has absolutely no emotional motivation to buy from you, the sale is simply not going to happen. By the same token, if we have absolutely no emotional motivation to take action on behalf of a prospect who wants to work with *us*, nothing's going to happen on that side, either.

> *How and why* **do the emotional buttons get pushed in the first place? Once we understand that much, we may be in a** better position **to** avoid **communication problems with our prospects.**

The decision to take action on something will *always* emerge from the realm of emotion first, and will typically connect to a pain we are trying to avoid or a pleasure we are eager to experience. Like Brett, we may use "intellectual" reasons to justify a decision to take action or to reject that action.

The question remains, though: *How and why do the emotional buttons get pushed in the first place?* Once we understand that much, we may be in a better position to avoid communication problems with our prospects. Let's consider how Sandler's emotion-driven decision-making process works in our own world.

Your Emotions Affect Your Decisions

When we say humans are emotionally driven animals, we're really saying that certain very strong feelings—feelings connected to internal messages such as "I feel free!" or "You betrayed me!" or "I love it!"—*begin* the decision-making process. That's true for us. It's also true for our prospects. It's true for everyone.

In *The Sandler Rules*, I talked at length about how that emotional dimension affects the *prospect's* decisions. Here, I want to look at a different issue. *How do you make* your *decisions—and why?* The answer to that pivotal question resides in the *choices* you make about the emotional messages you allow to control your behavior.

Once you understand how your own emotions work, and where your strongest emotional messages are likely to come from, you're in a much better position to communicate effectively with clients, customers, and prospects. Once you understand what's really behind your own decisions, you can help others make good decisions, too.

David Sandler, following the lead of Dr. Eric Berne, author of the landmark book *Games People Play: The Psychology of Human Relationships*, saw that salespeople, prospects, and everyone else's actions—including decisions—are profoundly influenced by three distinct ego states—each a system of thoughts and feelings and corresponding patterns of behavior. Dr. Berne defined these ego states as the Parent, the Adult, and the Child.

As a person, you really are a *group* of individuals: a Parent, an Adult, and a Child. Understanding these three ways of looking at the world, and how they interact within you, will help you get a clearer understanding of the emotions you're feeling at any given moment and the decisions you're making in response to those emotions—not only in selling, but in any number of other areas in your life, as well.

Figure 6.1: Ego State Tapes

Three Ego States, Three Tape Recorders

It may come as a surprise to you to learn that your brain has been carefully recording *virtually everything of emotional significance* that has happened to you since early childhood. Surprising though it is, it is true. Every influence, every important discussion, every experience that evoked some kind of powerful emotion within you is all recorded somewhere within your memory. These memories may not be conscious, or easily accessible, but they are there, and they are influencing you all the time.

Your **Parent ego state** is one tape recorder. ("There are going to be consequences for doing this. Stop and think.")

Your **Adult ego state** is another tape recorder. ("When you say 'X,' what do you mean?")

Your **Child ego state** is the third tape recorder. ("I want it . . . now!")

> **Whenever we listen to our** Child or Parent **recordings, we are likely to be replaying those recordings** without realizing that **that is what we are doing, and without evaluating how** relevant **the tapes are to the situation we are facing at the** time.

Dr. Berne and other researchers were able to confirm that these three "tape recorders" are what replay the hundreds of thousands of stored memories that allow us to function. *The recordings may be ancient, but they continue to have massive influences on our day-to-day lives.* In the words of Thomas Harris, author of the landmark best seller *I'm OK, You're OK,* which drew heavily on Dr. Berne's work:

> [Even] our earliest experiences, though [wordless], are recorded, and do replay in the present. . . . If all experiences and feelings are recorded, we can understand the extreme panic, or fear, or rage we feel in certain situations today as a reliving of the original state . . . We can think of this as a *replay* of the original tape.

This metaphor about replaying an old recording is not a gimmick or a literary trick. It's the fundamental reality of the human condition— your condition and my condition. At any given moment, when left to our own deepest instincts, we are, in all likelihood, replaying reactions we learned at a very deep level, years ago. Whenever we listen to our Child or Parent recordings, we are likely to be replaying those recordings without realizing that that is what we are doing, and without evaluating how relevant the tapes are to the situation we are facing at the time.

> **The recordings that we play most often help to form our life script—our basic set of operating assumptions about the world.**

The recordings that we play most often help to form our **life script**—our basic set of operating assumptions about the world. We tend to reinforce our own life script over time. There is only one way to become aware of the contents of the life script and change it: we must become better at noticing what we are replaying and why we are replaying it.

With that in mind, let's look at all three of the ego states in more depth.

Parent

The Parent ego state recorder was running for approximately the first five years of your life. The tape in this recorder contains all the "how-to's" passed along to you by your mother, father, and other authority figures in your life. This information has been *permanently recorded* onto this tape. It cannot be altered or erased. This tape plays on a regular basis inside your head, and most of the time it either issues instructions ("Do this"; "Don't do that") or issues praise and support ("That's all right. You're still OK.")

On one side of that tape are the "rules and regulations," a collection of messages that you received from a figure, or group of figures, we call the Critical Parent. On the other side of that tape are the "warm and friendly" messages you got from the person, or group of people, we collectively call the Nurturing Parent.

Each of us has this tape. Each of us has messages from a Critical Parent that can—and do—play back in response to certain situations. Each of us also has messages from a Nurturing Parent that we may hear inside our head, and these messages, too, will replay during interactions with others.

Do you remember hearing any of the following when you were a young child?

"Finish your dinner or there will be no dessert."

"If you know what's good for you, you'll listen to me."

"There'll be no TV until you clean your room."

"You'll do what I tell you to do or else. . . ."

"I know what's best for you."

"Don't question me."

Sure you have. I'll bet you've made similar statements to your own children. **When you did, you were replaying messages from your Critical Parent.**

> **We wanted to be our own (little) person, to be free to make our own decisions, act the way we wanted to act, and think the way we wanted to think.**

As young children, we were frequently told what to do and when and how to do it. Sometimes, we were OK with what mom (or dad, grandma, Uncle Bill, Aunt Sally, etc.) told us. But, there were other times—perhaps many of them—when we were not OK. We didn't want to be told what to do. We wanted to be our own (little) person, to be free to make our own decisions, act the way we wanted to act, and think the way we wanted to think.

What happened when mom intruded on that freedom with those Critical Parent messages? Sometimes, we happily complied with her wishes. Other times, we begrudgingly adhered to her directives. There were also times when we stomped off to our room in protest.

By telling us what to do, mom was teaching us the difference between right and wrong, good and bad, and appropriate and inappropriate behavior. At some level, we probably knew that she cared about us and was acting in our best interest, even if we didn't acknowledge it at the time. Her actions were recorded and filed away in our subconscious whether we agreed with them or not.

> **Both Critical Parent and Nurturing Parent messages have the potential to influence our behavior during interactions with others.**

We still carry those "recordings" today, just as we carry messages from the Nurturing Parent in our lives, messages that tells things such as:

"You're going to be OK."

"It's all right. Everyone makes mistakes."

"You're still my best boy/girl."

Both Critical Parent and Nurturing Parent messages have the potential to influence our behavior during interactions with others. This usually happens when we are trying to make a point about what is right and wrong, good and bad, appropriate and inappropriate.

Child

There was something else going on when mom was telling us what to do. We were generating *feelings* about the encounter and recording them on the Child ego state recorder, which also ran for the first five years of our lives. When we were OK with the situation, we generated positive feelings, such as happiness, delight, and acceptance. When we were not OK with the situation, we were apt to generate opposite feelings—sadness, anger, or possibly rejection. Those feelings were also filed away, ready for the Child part of our personality—the most creative and spontaneous of our three ego states—to replay when we encountered situations similar to the ones in which they were generated.

Thus, the messages on the Child ego state tape are often driven by powerful emotions. **You are expressing feelings that were recorded in your Child ego state when you find yourself spouting out, "Don't tell me what to do!" or "Fantastic!" or "I don't care!" or "I want it now!"**

> **The Child in you can take different forms . . . Remember that all kinds of responses from this tape are *feeling-driven* responses to the "rules of the road" that we heard from our parents and recorded on our Parent tape recorder.**

No matter how much your parents nurtured you during your first five or so years of life, you still developed a lot of not-OK feelings about yourself. Almost everyone was bigger than you and there was very little you could do for yourself—you depended on others to attend to your needs. And when you expressed your natural urges to explore, to know, to bang things, and to express feelings, you often discovered that you had to suppress them in order to obtain parental approval. The by-product of those frustrating situations was negative feelings. You still carry around a lot of these archaic, not-OK feelings. If you didn't, you wouldn't have a functioning emotional system! The trick is not to *get rid* of archaic feelings—that's impossible—but rather to *notice where they are coming from*.

The Child in you can take different forms (those forms will be explained in later chapters). For now, just remember that all kinds of responses from this tape are *feeling-driven* responses to the "rules of the road" that we heard from our parents and recorded on our Parent tape recorder.

Adult

The Adult ego state recorder began taping when you were about one year old, and is *the only tape recorder still recording new material*. It is objective, rational, non-opinionated, and non-prejudicial. It is the part of you that solves problems unemotionally by processing facts and making rational decisions.

> The Adult ego state recorder began taping when you were about one year old, and is *the only tape recorder* *still recording* *new* *material*.

We may have convinced ourselves that the only state that matters is the Adult ego state, but the fact is that the Parent and the Child ego states are likely to play profound roles in our lives. **The job of the Adult is to filter information coming from the outside world, listening to feedback from the Parent and the Child.**

You must decide if you are willing to listen to your Adult as it evaluates the messages from the Parent and the Child to determine whether those messages are still appropriate or whether they are outdated.

Take Control!

If you want to take control of your own world, you need only determine which ego state is operating at any given moment and what message it is sending out. You need only learn to examine the tapes that are running in your mind, and start noticing whether the tape recorders are sending messages that are relevant about whether you, and/or those around you, are fundamentally "OK" or "not-OK."

Of course, it would be nice if we all stopped making choices based on archaic information from our Parent and Child tape recorders the minute we became "legal" adults. Most of us, however, continue long after the age of eighteen to make emotionally fueled decisions that incorporate outdated information and assumptions from our Parent and Child recordings. Yes, that goes for prospects, but it goes for us, too.

The ability to distinguish instantly between what is and is not still relevant from the old recordings is not something we can expect to master overnight. We can, however, get better at this skill over time based on how much attention we pay to what the old tapes are saying and what's actually happening in the situations we face in life.

The better we are at noticing what drove decisions that were made years ago, the better we will get at making new decisions, and the more persuasive models we will be as decision makers for our prospects.

Let Your Adult Take Center Stage

With time and practice, you will find that you can develop a greater degree of internal control by letting your Adult "take center stage" more often. This will enable you to maintain an objective perspective through which you can filter your experiences and reframe your communications with others.

> **When we bring the Adult into the conversation, letting it take center stage, we take advantage of an ego state that is straightforward in action, generates objective feedback, and monitors what's actually happening in the real world.**

We cannot turn the tape recorders off, but we can learn to step back and listen to the recordings that we are playing. We can determine their origin. And we can find ways to cultivate a healthy Adult assessment of the messages we are receiving from the Parent and Child recorders. When we bring the Adult into the conversation, letting it take center stage, we take advantage of an ego state that is straightforward in action, generates objective feedback, and monitors what's actually happening in the real world. By doing so, we can help ourselves and others to make any necessary adjustments. This is what Sandler wanted us to know about human decision making: *It is inevitably* driven *by the Child's emotional response, scrutinized by the Parent, and evaluated by the Adult ego state.*

In «««
Summary

Many decisions—not only buying decisions—begin with the Child ego state.

The feelings stored on our Child tape drive our desire or impulse to buy, to have, to do, to avoid, to become, to experience, and to achieve.

When we allow our Parent and Adult to review and sign off on a decision, we are more comfortable with it and not likely to have second thoughts.

Time for
REFLECTION ‹‹ ‹‹ ‹‹

Think About Your Buying Decisions

All buying decisions are emotionally driven even if the *need* to buy is an intellectual one. For example, the decision to replace a broken cell phone may be an intellectual one since the phone is an integral business tool that increases your efficiency and productivity. But, the ultimate buying decision—which phone, in which color, with which features, and with which accessories—will be an emotional one.

» Think of some recent items you purchased. They could be major purchases such as a car, a computer, or a piece of furniture. Or, they could be minor purchases, such as a book or magazine, a music CD or movie DVD, or items you picked up at the grocery store.

» For each of the recent items you listed above, identify the Child influence on the purchase decision.

  » Was it a Child impulse that initiated the purchase?

  » Did the Child take over after the need for the purchase was identified?

  » What emotion—greed, envy, desire, fears, etc.—had the greatest influence?

  » Did you have to "justify" the purchase after the fact? If so, did you reveal your Child impulses or did you provide a more "intellectual" explanation?

7

>>>> Seventy percent of your selling behavior comes from your Nurturing Parent.

"**O**ur servers have crashed six times in the past thirty days," Bill told Marcia, the salesperson, exasperated. "Frankly, I don't think anybody's servers are capable of true reliability, but your equipment couldn't possibly be any worse than what we have now."

"That sounds really frustrating, Bill," Marcia said. "I can only imagine the pressure you were under to get the servers back up and running."

"You have no idea," Bill said. "Let me tell you what we're looking for . . ."

Marcia's response to Bill's frustration about his computer system could have made use of any one of the three ego state tape recorders operating in her psyche. She chose the Nurturing track of the Parent, saying, "That sounds really frustrating . . ."

> ## Of the three ego states you learned about in Principle 6, the Nurturing aspect of the Parent is the one that is most likely to initiate good transactions.

Consider what she *didn't* say, but could have:

"Well, if you had invested in servers that have a documented 99+ percent up-time like ours do, you never would have had reliability problems." (Critical Parent)

"Honestly, I can't understand why we're even meeting if you aren't willing to admit that our equipment *could* be reliable." (Child)

Marcia chose to respond by adapting the Nurturing Parent messages she had on her own tape. As a result, she supported a good exchange—a good *transaction*—with Bill.

Of the three ego states you learned about in Principle 6, the Nurturing aspect of the Parent is the one that is most likely to initiate good transactions. This facet of the ego state launches *most* of the successful salesperson's communication with prospects and customers. In fact, David Sandler advised that we should aim to spend 70 percent of our selling time in Nurturing Parent mode.

> **It's not surprising that prospective buyers would respond well to the Nurturing Parent's messages and tend to open up to a productive discussion after hearing those messages.**

The Nurturing Parent, you'll remember, is the Parent who reassures, comforts, and supports. This Parent is agreeable, approachable, and positive. It's not surprising that prospective buyers would respond well to the Nurturing Parent's messages and tend to open up to a productive discussion after hearing those messages.

The emotionally supportive messages that arise from the Nurturing Parent tape can take many forms, including supporting body language and facial expressions that encourage the other person to speak, and statements such as:

"We've seen this kind of issue before."

"A lot of your counterparts in this industry have reported having this kind of issue."

"Those are admirable goals."

"That's my feeling as well."

"I understand your frustration."

"That must have been a very difficult period for your company. Let's see what we can do to make sure it doesn't happen again."

Of course, when we send these messages, we have to be certain that we are doing so in a way that is both authentic and respectful. (Sarcasm is *never* a message from the Nurturing Parent.) If our communications meet those standards, we will find that, more often than not, our messages open doors and make productive transactions with our prospects possible.

Why do you think our prospects and customers are likely to respond well to these kinds of messages? Why are these signals so effective at helping people to open up? Here's one answer: People respond positively to us after hearing these messages not just because the words we choose are apt, and not just because the tone of voice or the facial expressions we use seem appropriate to the situation, but also because of the powerful feelings and memories these supportive messages evoke.

> **Positive human responses to authentic, respectful Nurturing Parent messages are likely to be *replays* of similar feelings we felt as kids. . . .**

Positive human responses to authentic, respectful Nurturing Parent messages are likely to be *replays* of similar feelings we felt as kids, decades ago, while our Parent and Child tape recorders were still taking in new information and we had the experience of being soothed by one of our own parents. Can you think of someone who played that Nurturing Parent role for you? (It doesn't have to be a biological parent.)

As children, when we fell down and hurt ourselves, or we found ourselves sick in bed, or touched something hot by mistake, what happened? If we were lucky, our Nurturing Parent was around at those moments and said things that reassured us, such as:

"I know how you feel."

"Where does it hurt?"

"You'll be OK."

"Don't worry."

"It's going to be all right."

"Let me kiss it and make it better."

When we encountered those messages as children, we felt certain kinds of powerful, positive responses, including feelings of comfort, validation, acceptance, being cared for, belonging, and safety. In short, we felt *OK*.

From this point forward, I'm going to call those kinds of emotions **OK Emotions**. Why? Because they are emotions that make us feel OK. People are more likely to interact effectively, and communicate better, when they feel OK. That's a reliable principle. It holds true for our prospects, and it holds true for us, too.

The ability to evoke OK Emotions is a major bonding tool.

As salespeople, we should constantly bear in mind what David Sandler was really telling us with this principle: that the ability to evoke OK Emotions is a major bonding tool. We will evoke these emotions most effectively during our interactions with prospects and customers when we do what Marcia did: communicate primarily with messages adapted from the Nurturing Parent tape.

There is likely to be a very different emotional response, of course, to messages that arise from the other side of the Parent tape—the side that has messages from the Critical Parent. I'll talk about those responses in the next chapter.

In «««
Summary

Nurturing Parent messages are likely to evoke OK Emotions in the other person.

People are more likely to interact effectively, and communicate better with each other, when they feel OK.

Time for
REFLECTION

Your Nurturing Parent Influence

Identify at least one specific exchange—one *transaction*—with an adult that went smoothly because you chose, either consciously or unconsciously, to play a message from your Nurturing Parent tape recorder. For example: Have you ever told a friend in crisis that everything would be all right? Have you ever told a customer that you would be frustrated if you were experiencing what he or she was experiencing?

>>> **Zero percent of your selling behavior comes from your Critical Parent.**

John, a sales representative for Detail Dental Lab, discovered from (painful) direct experience the truth of this principle.

A little background first: Detail Dental Lab (DDL) makes customized crowns, bridges, inlays, dentures, veneers, and other dental appliances. The company has been in business for over thirty years, and has earned an outstanding reputation among dentists for handling cases in which a patient's dental trauma has been extreme.

About a month ago, John was calling on Dr. Maurice Silver for the first time. Dr. Silver is the owner of a relatively new dental practice that specializes in restorative dentistry. Even though Dr. Silver was using another lab in town, and was relatively happy with their work, he agreed to meet with John. He was familiar with DDL and was open to discussing the types of restoration cases he customarily handled.

Up to that moment, John believed the meeting marked the beginning of a new and lucrative business relationship. Now, he sat alone, wondering what had just happened.

John thought the meeting was going exceptionally well. He and the doctor discussed the importance of controlling thermal expansion of PFM bridges during the firing process, the pros and cons of using composite crowns, and the latest advances in foil veneers. Dr. Silver was thoroughly impressed with John's knowledge. He asked John several questions about the company's policies, pricing, and turnaround times for specific types of work. He appeared comfortable with John's answers. About thirty minutes into the meeting, Dr. Silver said to John, "Perhaps I should see what your lab can do."

John suggested that the doctor let DDL handle the next restoration case requirements, if only as a trial, to demonstrate the exceptional work and service his firm could provide. Dr. Silver agreed. Feeling particularly confident, John promised Dr, Silver, "Once you see the quality work we do, you'll be giving us *all* of your work. I can assure you, you won't have a need for another lab."

The doctor sat silent for a moment, looking directly at John. His smile slowly changed to a blank stare. Then he stood up, told John to leave his card with the receptionist, and walked out of the room.

Up to that moment, John believed the meeting marked the beginning of a new and lucrative business relationship. Now, he sat alone, wondering what had just happened.

Perhaps, he thought, the doctor had suddenly remembered something pressing to which he had to attend. Without giving the matter any further thought, he did as he had been instructed and gave his business card to Melissa, the receptionist, along with a new account application form for the doctor to complete. He also left behind a pad of Rx lab slips.

"Talk to you soon, Melissa," he said on his way out, still feeling quite confident about the deal.

> **Even though those people were** looking out **for us, and they presumably had our best interests at** heart**, we simply didn't like** being told **what to do.**

Several weeks passed. John heard nothing from Dr. Silver, nor did he receive a new account application. When John phoned the doctor, he was never able to reach him directly, and his calls were never returned.

Perhaps you're asking yourself the same question John kept asking himself in the weeks after that meeting: What happened? To find a possible explanation, let's revisit the Critical Parent we discussed in an earlier chapter.

During early childhood, we were often told what to do, and how and when to do it, by our parents and other authority figures. Sometimes, we were OK with what we heard; other times, perhaps frequently, we were not so OK. Even though those people were looking out for us, and they presumably had our best interests at heart, we simply didn't like being told what to do. Like most children, we wanted to behave the way *we* wanted to, not the way someone else *told* us to behave. Even when the behavior they described was essentially what we would have done on our own anyway, we still didn't like being told what to do.

If, as a child, you were not particularly pleased when your mom told you what to do and what was best for you—even when she had persuasive reasons for believing that it was for your own good—then you probably don't like it today when people tell you what to do or what is best for you. You may not stomp off to your room, but you will find a way to channel your discomfort!

Could anything we've learned about the Critical Parent ego state explain Dr. Silver's behavior? Let's find out.

As it happened, John wasn't ready to give up the challenge of obtaining Dr. Silver's business. He wrote him a letter—not an e-mail, but an actual letter. He wrote:

Dear Dr. Silver,

It's been a few weeks since our meeting and I haven't heard from you. I've been unsuccessful in reaching out to you by phone and you haven't returned any of my calls. I have to believe that you are no longer interested in determining the value Detail Dental Lab can bring to your practice. I'm sure you have a good reason.

Losing a potential client, however, is like losing a friend; I wouldn't let either drift away in silence. If it's something I've said or done, I'd like to know. I don't want to make the same mistake again. I really do care and would like to know what, if anything, I can do to make it right.

I would consider it a favor if you would take my call on Thursday at 8 AM and let me know what happened. If 8 AM is not convenient, could you please have Melissa inform me of a better time?

Sincerely,

John Salzmann

John made the call on Thursday morning, as promised. To his surprise, Dr. Silver himself answered the phone. He told John that he appreciated the extra effort reflected in John writing a personal letter. He admitted that he was impressed with John's knowledge and equally impressed by Detail Dental Lab's reputation for precision work. However, he further revealed, he *wasn't* impressed with John's attitude at the end of their meeting.

He explained, "I didn't appreciate your little lecture, telling me how to run my practice and telling me that I'd be giving you all of my lab work. You undoubtedly know that there are over a dozen labs in the city. I can give as much or as little work to whichever labs I choose. I don't need you telling me what to do."

> **During that first meeting, he had made a classic selling mistake: letting his Critical Parent determine the direction of a conversation.**

John's first thought was to tell the doctor that he had been overly sensitive and had overreacted. If Dr. Silver honestly believed that John was telling him how to run his practice, maybe Dr. Silver ought to take a deep breath, relax, and think back to what had actually taken place during the meeting! (*What do you suppose would have happened if John had said any of that to Dr. Silver?*)

Fortunately, John stopped himself in time. He realized that it was *the act of "telling"*—what the doctor characterized as a lecture— that had gotten him into trouble in the first place. During that first meeting, he had made a classic selling mistake: letting his Critical Parent determine the direction of a conversation.

John resisted the instinct to correct the doctor, and said the following instead: "Doctor Silver, I understand your feelings. I suppose if the tables were turned, I'd feel the same way. Sometimes, I let my enthusiasm get the best of me. You see, I've worked for DDL for over seventeen years. I started working there as a lab technician when I was in college and have performed almost every job in the company.

"In our industry, there are plenty of shortcuts that can be taken while still turning out an *acceptable* product. However, it is DDL's commitment to turn out *superior* products, not just acceptable ones. That means no shortcuts . . . ever.

> **If you're looking for a reliable way to make a prospect feel *not-OK*, keep your Critical Parent tape playing all the time.**

"I sensed that you would appreciate that and would want to work with a lab with that philosophy—specifically, our lab. Obviously, I did a very poor job of expressing that. I apologize for my poor choice of words."

The doctor accepted John's apology and committed to sending some work his way. It was a little over a month before that happened. Evidently, it took the doctor some time to put aside his feelings about "being told what to do."

In «« Summary

If you're looking for a reliable way to make a prospect feel *not-OK*, keep your Critical Parent tape playing all the time. Tell the other person what should happen, what he or she should do, and what's right and wrong, appropriate and inappropriate, good and bad about his or her decisions, opinions, and actions.

Don't be surprised when the prospect decides to put a stop to the *not-OK feelings* by putting a stop to communications with you.

Time for
REFLECTION ⟪ ⟪ ⟪
Your Critical Parent Influence

Lecturing to a prospect or customer, or even sounding as though you are lecturing, may earn you the honor of being dismissed, either figuratively or literally, by the prospect.

≫ Why not take a moment now to reflect on your recent interactions with prospects and customers?

　≫ Were there any times when your interactions could have been characterized as "telling" the prospect what he or she should or shouldn't be doing?

　≫ Were there any exchanges in which you could have been perceived as explaining what was good for the prospect and what wasn't?

　≫ For each instance, reframe the interaction using language that is more nurturing. Rather than using phrases such as "Let me tell you . . ." or "Here's what you should do . . ." for example, could you consider reframing the statement as a question? For instance: "Would it be helpful if . . .?" or "Can you see any benefit in . . .?"

≫≫≫ **Thirty percent of your selling behavior comes from your Adult.**

Mark, a consultant who specialized in text development and intellectual-property creation, received an unexpected phone call yesterday. He had hardly picked up the phone and said the words "Hello, this is Mark," when he heard a stream of words rushing from the other end of the line. He almost felt as though he had interrupted someone else's conversation.

"Right! Hiya, Mark, my name's Brian Barkham, president of BrainMarkers Industries," said the gruff voice on the other end of the line, quite rapidly. "I was just talking to Nellie Toddman, one of your clients, and she told me that she had a really great experience with you on the Toddman Kickoff Training manual. I want you to do the same kind of work for us, and I know you're going to do just as great a job for our company. How do we get started? What do we do first? Contracts, I suppose. Can you fax me your standard contract? By the way, I need this yesterday. How much do you want to get started and where do I send the check?"

He tried to bring some structure—and a voice of patience, reason, and experience— to the conversation.

Mark had been in business for himself for a while, so he knew better than to respond in kind by simply asking for the BrainMarkers Industries fax number and sending the standard contract along with a list of fees. Instead, he tried to bring some structure—and a voice of patience, reason, and experience—to the conversation.

"I'm very glad you called, Mr. Barkham, and I'm certainly happy that Nellie connected us. Have you got a couple of minutes to chat now, or should we set up another time to talk about your project?"

"Sure! Let's go ahead and talk now, Mark," said Mr. Barkham. "I need help from a great writer to create a great manual for an upcoming training session, and from everything Nellie mentioned about your work, you're exactly the person I want to be working with. Pardon the noise, by the way, I'm driving to a meeting of my board of directors, and I've got the convertible top down. Anyway, we've got plenty of time to talk. I've got ten whole minutes before the meeting starts. I do want to get started ASAP, though. So what's the bottom line on our project, anyway? How much is this going to cost me?"

"I'd love to be able to tell you that right now, Mr. Barkham," said Mark, "but before I try to, I think it's probably a good idea for us to talk for just a couple of minutes about the kind of project we're looking at. That way I can find out what you're looking for, learn about the scope of the project, get a sense of the timeline you're looking at, and get a better idea of whether or not this makes sense for us to pursue together. Can I start by asking you what your company does and what the purpose of the training session is going to be?"

When Mark stepped back from the rushing rapids of Brian's "let's do it now!" monologue, and asked what Brian's company did and what the purpose of the training was going to be, he was letting his Adult do the talking. The Adult, you'll remember, is the ego state tape recorder that began taping when you were about one year old and is the *only* recorder still taking in new information.

Following David Sandler's lead, our aim should be to make roughly 30 percent of our sales interactions start with an Adult assessment of issues.

Whereas Brian's impulsive, powerful message issued primarily from the Child recorder, Mark knew that, at some point, logic, reason, evaluation, recent experience, and objectivity were going to have to come into play, not only on Brian's side, but on his side, too.

Did it really make sense for Brian and Mark to do business together? There was absolutely no way to know the answer to that question without posing some good questions and evaluating the answers together. By taking the lead and posing those questions, Mark tapped into the part of himself that solves problems unemotionally by gathering and assessing all the facts and making objective, rational decisions based on the best available information.

Whether the Child message we receive from the prospect or customer seems positive or negative at the time, we must not reciprocate with Child messages of our own, such as, "Sure! Let's get started!" Following David Sandler's lead, our aim should be to make roughly 30 percent of our sales interactions start with an Adult assessment of issues such as these:

» Is there the potential here for a good match?

» What exactly are we trying to accomplish?

» By what benchmarks will the success or failure of the project be determined?

» What are the ideal timelines?

» What is the size and scope of the project?

» What are the resources available? (Is there a budget on the prospect's side to do this? Is there space in the schedule and inventory to complete the project to the prospect's satisfaction?)

» Is this really something we can do well?

> **By asking** good questions **and conducting** responsible **investigations in the Adult mode about what the project actually was and whether it truly** made sense **for both sides, Mark was conducting an** essential **early reality check that laid the** groundwork **for what proved, eventually, to be a** mutually rewarding **project.**

Mark knew from experience that a prospect like Brian was capable of "falling out of love" with a prospective vendor just as quickly as he was capable of "falling in love" with that same vendor. He also knew that someone at Brian's company—either Brian or someone on his staff—would eventually start posing the pragmatic, problem-solving questions of the Adult ego state in order to justify Brian's intense desire to "do something now" and "get started immediately." Mark wanted to begin that evaluative process himself, and he wanted to begin it sooner rather than later. Why? Because he knew that the sale would begin emotionally and (as we have seen) ultimately be *confirmed and justified* with logic.

By asking good questions and conducting responsible investigations in the Adult mode about what the project actually was and whether it truly made sense for both sides, Mark was conducting an essential early reality check that laid the groundwork for what proved, eventually, to be a mutually rewarding project.

> He knew that the sale would begin emotionally and (as we have seen) ultimately be *confirmed and justified* with logic.

If he'd simply followed the dictates of Brian's Child by naming a figure out of thin air and faxing over the standard contract as ordered, who knows what would have happened? The same conversation could have played out with one of Mark's competitors the very next day, and Mark, flying blind, might have lost the business!

In Summary

Salespeople have been told to be enthusiastic and show excitement and passion when discussing their product or service. That's good advice, if it's applied at the appropriate time in the selling cycle—usually during the presentation phase.

A good part of the qualifying phase requires the collection of data—cold, hard facts—to fully define the opportunity. That requires a more pragmatic approach—an Adult approach.

Time for

REFLECTION

Your Adult Influence

Think of the last deal you actually closed.

» Who was spending the most time in Adult mode during the discussions that led up to the close, you or your prospect?

» What were some examples of your own Adult influence in this sale?

10

>>>> **Zero percent of your selling behavior comes from your Child.**

C al, a new salesperson who found himself performing just under quota for about one year, had been working with a senior decision maker within a Fortune 1000 organization for four months. Cal believed, after half-a-dozen meetings with a variety of key people at the company, that he had made significant progress within the account. During a meeting with his primary contact, however, he heard something he didn't expect.

Cal's contact said, "I should tell you that I think I may have to review our vendor options here."

This was pure betrayal, and it definitely wasn't the way Cal wanted to operate!

Cal's stomach began churning. Only last week, as a result of all those in-depth interviews Cal had done and all the hard work he had put into his proposed solution, this prospect had *clearly* told him that his two chief competitors had been excluded from the deal! His exact words were that Cal now had the "inside track" to create the program they were discussing. Nothing on Cal's side had changed, but obviously one of his competitors had found some way to go over his head and steal the business away despite his contact's earlier commitment, and despite all of Cal's hard work. *Now*, Cal thought to himself bitterly, *I'm going to fall even further behind quota because I connected with an unethical decision maker.* This was pure betrayal, and it definitely wasn't the way Cal wanted to operate!

"I hope you realize," Cal blurted out, "that if you do 'review your vendor options,' you'll be going back on your word. You said that I had the *inside track* on this deal. Is this how you do business?"

The meeting went downhill from there; in fact, the business relationship ended as soon as the meeting did!

Let's fast-forward exactly one year to the day after that disastrous meeting. Cal was talking to *another* Fortune 1000 prospect, operating in a different industry. Yet again, Cal had invested months of work in the relationship and had done a great job; yet again, his prospect had excluded the competition and promised Cal the inside track. And then, the prospect, a senior vice president named Dianne, threw Cal the same curveball: "Hmm, I think I'm going to have to review my vendor options here, Cal."

The same surge of emotion rushed through Cal's system: this was another betrayal!

Cal quickly moved past it. Instead of reacting, Cal *responded*. This time, he said, "Dianne, can you help me out with something? When you say 'review your vendor options,' *what exactly do you mean*?"

Dianne explained: "Well, when we met last week, you told me that we were going to have to think about the schedule soon, because your inventory capacity was going to be stretched thin over the next ninety days."

Instead of reacting, Cal *responded*.

While technically true (because inventory was always a potential problem) this was also a common ploy Cal used to introduce immediacy and urgency into the final phases of the sales cycle. He recalled that he'd used the same urgency tactic on the other Fortune 1000 account, as well.

"I remember," said Cal.

"The problem is, my CEO has put me in a bind. He's reduced my budget line, which means I have to get his sign-off. He's out of the country on vacation until next week. At the same time, he's sending me e-mails that are putting me under some pretty intense time pressure," Dianne explained. "So if we can't make all this happen within the next ninety days, I'm going to have to start thinking about building some other vendors into this solution. I'd want you to take the lead over the life of the project, and, ideally, I'd rather make you the sole vendor, of course, but at this point that really depends on the schedule we can get from you."

"Suppose we found a way to get our CEOs on the phone together for a short conference call next week?" Cal asked. "If we can commit to that, I could talk to my CEO and buy us some more time for you to make your decision *and* hold on to your schedule."

"Great. Let's do it," Dianne said.

Who Was in Charge?

In the first conversation, Cal was under the sway of his Child tape. He acted on his powerful feelings of betrayal by venting. That didn't exactly deliver the outcome he was after, did it?

One year after that, Cal *chose* to move past the Child tape. (He also chose to move past the Critical Parent tape, which would have delivered an equally unsatisfying result.) His choice led to a very different conversation, one that was focused on establishing what actually mattered to his prospect, and what really was (and wasn't) working in the real world.

> If we don't "leave the Child in the car" when we make a sales call, we may react inappropriately to a seeming obstacle . . . or we may seek to win the buyer's approval in ways that really don't help either party.

Cal never learned to turn off the Child tape recorder—none of us do. But he did learn to *decide when it didn't make sense to play it out loud for the world to hear.* Relying on his old Child tape was damaging his relationships with his prospects.

When we look at Cal's two conversations, we can understand why David Sandler was so insistent about leaving the Child ego state *out* of our exchanges with prospects and customers. If we don't "leave the Child in the car" when we make a sales call, we may react inappropriately to a seeming obstacle, as Cal did in the first conversation, or we may seek to win the buyer's approval in ways that really don't help either party.

Simply *knowing* this principle is not enough. We must *practice* "leaving our Child in the car." Most salespeople don't practice this enough, and as a result, they sabotage—in an instant—relationships they've invested weeks, months, or years in developing!

> **Simply *knowing* this principle is not enough. We must *practice* "leaving our Child in the car."**

In ≪≪≪ Summary

Cal only started making good decisions about how to respond to his prospect *once he learned to listen more to his Adult and Nurturing Parent tapes than to his Child tapes.*

He was never able to eliminate the Child recorder's messages entirely, of course. They were too deeply imbedded. But he did figure out *which messages were no longer supporting him during his exchanges with clients.*

Once he had done that, he could "leave the Child in the car," and look for ways to communicate from his Nurturing Parent, or, as in this case, operate on the Adult assumption that new information, analysis, and discussion were the best response when faced with what seemed, at first, to be an incomprehensible objection.

Time for
REFLECTION
Your Child Influence

» Can you think of a time when a response from your Child tape cost you a deal or nearly cost you a deal?

  » What would you do and say differently now?

11

>>> **If you are only what you were told you could be, you are less than what you can be.**

We all face a sobering truth: Our deepest, most instinctive responses are inevitably products of our upbringing.

Even more sobering is this truth: Our very personalities—our characters—were shaped during early childhood by the messages we received and the behaviors we observed from our parents and the other adult authority figures in our world. Those modeled patterns of behavior and the feelings generated by the messages we received were all recorded and are stored within us, ready for replay at any time. Whether we wish to acknowledge the fact or not, the messages and feelings of our very early years were the starting point of our attitudes, our beliefs about our abilities, and, ultimately, our path in life.

Some people grew up in highly supportive environments where they frequently heard statements such as this: "You can be anything you want to be if you put your mind to it" and "If you work hard, you can accomplish anything." Others grew up in environments where the messages were far less supportive. These messages may have been more along the lines of: "You'll never amount to anything," "You're a loser," and "Why try? You'll only fail again." There are many sad cases of people whose parents always told them things such as, "I swear, you're going to end up in prison someday." Tragically, many of them did.

> **Whether we wish to** acknowledge **the fact or not, the messages and feelings of our** very early years **were the starting point of our attitudes, our beliefs about our abilities, and, ultimately, our** path in life.

Perhaps you're wondering: Do the people who were brought up in the most supportive environments *automatically* develop healthy self-esteem and become successful? Are those whose environments were less supportive *destined* to develop poor self-images and become the failures the messages they recorded suggest?

The answer to both questions is "no."

We have all heard stories about people who grew up under the very worst circumstances—with abusive, unsupportive parents, with teachers who wrote them off at an early age, with friends who made every effort to hold them back from any meaningful accomplishment—and who still found a way to live lives that were successful by anyone's standards, lives full of contribution and achievement. We've also heard plenty of true stories of people who grew up in supportive family environments who managed to live lives of misery and despair.

So, how do we account for the difference?

Like a bowling pin, which is a product of a manufacturing process that shapes it into its recognizable form, you, too, are a product of a process that has shaped your behavior and actions into a recognizable form.

We can start by acknowledging that people don't lead a "bowling pin" existence. Bowling pins have no choice but to fall over when hit by a bowling ball. It's the way they were built. It's their destiny to be knocked down, time and time again. Despite what some bowlers may tell you, the pins can't choose to stand their ground and refuse to fall when struck by the ball, and they will never choose a new strategy to move out of the way of a rapidly approaching ball to avoid being knocked over. They will never choose to abandon the unsafe environment of the bowling lane and seek a safer environment. Game after game, they will continue to fulfill their destiny, which is to be knocked down over and over and over again by every ball with which they come into contact.

Let me revise this slightly: people don't lead a bowling pin existence . . . unless they choose to. Like a bowling pin, which is a product of a manufacturing process that shapes it into its recognizable form, you, too, are a product of a process that has shaped your behavior and actions into a recognizable form. That shaping, or programming, was performed by your parents and other authority figures during your early childhood. They taught you, from their perspective, what was right and wrong, good and bad, appropriate and inappropriate. You may have obediently accepted their directives, rebelliously adopted a behavior opposite to what they taught, or exhibited a behavior somewhere between those two ends of the spectrum. **Regardless, you are a product of that upbringing, and what you feel, think, and do in the present is strongly influenced by it.**

> **You have the freedom to be, to do, to become, and to be known and remembered for whatever you want.**

Unlike a bowling pin, however, which has no choice but to carry out its designed behavior, you have free will. You can make choices about how you act and react to your programming. You can structure your life to strictly adhere to and validate that programming and the scripted behavior it describes, *or* you can choose to direct your energy to alternative behaviors that better serve you in the present. You have the freedom to be, to do, to become, and to be known and remembered for whatever you want.

The choice is yours.

How do you exercise this power of choice? Choosing a new path will likely require you to change your thinking. You can begin by recognizing that there is no right or wrong time to make a good choice, regardless of the choices you may have made in the past. Next, you must learn to stop paying attention to unsupportive childhood messages—principally, the Parent directives and Child emotions—that have exerted a negative controlling influence on your life. Finally, you must acknowledge your true goals and dreams as valid ones, even if they are counter to your programming.

Make New Choices and You Will Change Your Life

Never forget: If past choices and their associated behaviors have brought you to a place in your life where you are not happy, you have the power to make new choices! Regardless of how established your existing path may appear, you can choose to change it, right now. Take a new path; take a detour; go off-road if necessary. You are only stuck on your existing path to the degree that you believe you are.

Be advised, though: Even when you do make new choices to take your life in new directions, the old messages will still play. Those messages will make you very uncomfortable at times. You'll have doubts. You'll have fears. You'll be anxious. The good news is that the discomfort will eventually diminish as you grow more comfortable with the process of making your own decisions.

> **Charting a new direction means becoming determined by knowing *exactly* what you want to achieve by making the change you have in mind.**

Choosing a new direction in life is primarily an Adult process. It's your Adult ego state that is consciously engaged when you make a choice; it's your Adult that is filtering the messages from the Parent and Child, determining whether the behavior directed by those messages will take you closer to or further from the goal, and deciding when a new behavior is more appropriate.

Charting a new direction means becoming determined by knowing *exactly* what you want to achieve by making the change you have in mind. You must *picture* yourself reaching that goal, and return often to the picture of that achievement to reinforce yourself when old patterns reemerge.

You must also have a planned alternative behavior. This is a new, enjoyable behavior that will replace the existing "bowling pin" pattern and enable you to achieve the desired outcome.

To stay on track, it also helps to have a trusted person to act as your coach, cheerleader, and conscience. This should be someone who can help you stay focused and provide encouragement. Many people get help from co-workers, supervisors, or friends. Some people hire professional business coaches or trainers to work on these issues. Whoever you choose, you should be comfortable reaching out to this person on a regular basis.

Martha Changes Her Strategy

Martha was a sales representative for a well-known computer systems company working within the governmental applications division. She was conscientious and always attended to the business at hand. She had made contact with several mid-level managers in the department of labor and was very active in helping them to brainstorm solutions to a major problem of maintaining and updating their database of a particular segment of the labor force. She was instrumental in helping them design more useful forms of data identification, storage, and retrieval. She anticipated that her company's systems, which she identified, would be utilized when they went to solution. However, the decision maker found suitable alternatives that seemed less costly, and went with them.

This was not an uncommon experience for Martha. She would invest large amounts of time and energy helping prospects to find a solution, only to discover that when push came to shove she would not get the sale.

> **Later in life, Martha learned that when she did her best work and was helpful to those in high places, she was amply rewarded and did not have to demand those rewards or negotiate for them in advance.**

Growing up, Martha discovered that when she was mom's little helper around the house, voluntarily cleaning her room and putting her toys away, she received hugs and praise from her mom without having to ask or bargain for them beforehand. She obtained similar praise being the kindergarten teacher's unofficial helper, cleaning up after cut-and-paste projects.

Later in life, Martha learned that when she did her best work and was helpful to those in high places, she was amply rewarded and did not have to demand those rewards or negotiate for them in advance. In her first sales position, working for a pharmaceutical company, she had received high praise for her work as a drug detail provider at the doctor's-office level, where her primary job functions revolved around educating the doctors. She had come to the computer systems company to make more money, only to discover that she often fell short of quota and was barely making anything above her base rate. She knew something was wrong, but she couldn't understand what it was or what she could do about it.

With the help of a Sandler Training coach, Martha was able to see, for the first time, that she had a script, and was playing it out, time and time again, with her prospects.

He helped her develop a strategy to discover, early on in the selling process, whether the outcome of her *giving* would be in her best interest and inevitably lead to her *receiving* the sale.

Martha's script read something like this: "I must give in order to receive." That, she realized, was exactly what she had been doing: *giving* her knowledge to her prospects with the expectation of *receiving* their business in return. Unfortunately, she was neither stating her expectation up front, nor was she obtaining her prospects' commitments—up front—to direct the business her way.

Initially, Martha argued with her coach that stating her expectations shouldn't be necessary, because she was, in fact, providing a valuable service. The prospect, she argued, should recognize that and act accordingly. Her coach helped her realized that pleasing her parents and teachers was a different activity than pleasing her prospects—one that has different outcomes. He helped her develop a strategy to discover, early on in the selling process, whether the outcome of her *giving* would be in her best interest and inevitably lead to her *receiving* the sale. She could then make better choices as to when, where, and with whom to invest her time.

At first, Martha was very uncomfortable asking her prospects directly about their intentions. She feared that her prospects would perceive her as pushy, and a big knot materialized regularly in her stomach, as if to remind her of that.

Martha's prospects, however, were far less shocked by her new strategy than she had imagined. Eventually, with the support of her coach, the discomfort disappeared and Martha became quite skilled at prequalifying her prospects. She became rather selective about the people with whom she shared her knowledge. Her frustration decreased, and her sales soared.

Jeff Becomes a Decision Maker

Jeff sold telecommunications equipment. He had the highest closing percentage of all the salespeople in his division. His technical knowledge was unsurpassed. His ability to uncover a prospect's needs and develop an appropriate solution was exceptional.

He should have been the top producer in the company, but he wasn't.

While Jeff had the highest closing rate in his organization, he also had the longest selling cycle. Jeff could get to the proposal development stage with a prospective client rather quickly. However, it took him an inordinate amount of time to secure an actual buying decision. He allowed the sales process to drag on and on.

> ### Even though his closing percentage was, on average, 50 percent higher than the other salespeople, his colleagues were closing 33 percent more sales than he was!

Asking his prospects to make commitments and decisions was difficult for him. What other salespeople in his company were accomplishing in an average of thirty days—sometimes less—took Jeff two months to accomplish. So, even though his closing percentage was, on average, 50 percent higher than the other salespeople, his colleagues were closing 33 percent more sales than he was!

Jeff recognized that he needed to shorten his selling cycle. He was uncomfortable, however, "pushing people to act," or asking people to "make hasty decisions." (Those were his words.)

Why did he feel that way?

As a youngster, Jeff had always been in a hurry. He would rush through his chores, his homework—almost any activity. He remembered his mother describing him as having only one speed—*fast-forward*. He also remembered her continually telling him, "Slow down. Don't be in such a hurry." "When you're in a hurry," she warned, "you're bound to make mistakes."

When it came to making decisions, Jeff was given similar "slow down" advice from his father, who taught him that it was best to "sleep on it" before making big decisions. "After all," his father would say, "you don't want to make a bad decision." He never explained *why* a decision made without sleeping on it was bad . . . and Jeff never asked.

Archaic **childhood messages—"slow down" and "sleep on it"—were** working against him.

For young Jeff, the message was clear: Doing things quickly—especially making decisions quickly—was somehow always wrong. It was better to take things slowly and not make mistakes than to risk making bad decisions.

Jeff had been carrying that behavior script around with him since childhood. Making decisions—even decisions others might consider routine, such as which movie to see or which restaurant to go to—seemed to take him forever, and usually caused him distress. He felt compelled to take a bit more time to consider his options before making the decision. It is no wonder that Jeff was reluctant to press his prospects for decisions. Archaic childhood messages—"slow down" and "sleep on it"—were working against him. They had created a pattern of behavior—a script—that not only influenced Jeff's actions, but also enabled him to "understand" (that is, sympathize with) anyone who seemed to be exhibiting a similar pattern.

When Jeff went on sales calls, his script required that he take his mom and dad with him. Not literally, of course, but figuratively. They would stand silently in the corner of the room, observing him, and waiting for the perfect moment to offer their "help" whenever they thought it necessary to do so.

> ## The selling process is driven by a series of decisions. The more quickly those decisions are made, the shorter the selling cycle.

When Jeff thought about asking his prospects to commit to completing a task by a certain date in order to keep the sale moving forward, he would hear his mother whisper in his ear, "Now, Jeff, don't be in such a hurry." As a result, Jeff would not ask for the commitment. Jeff knew that the purpose of making any presentation was to obtain a buying decision, but the minute the prospect exhibited any hesitation or expressed the desire to give the decision some additional thought, Jeff felt his dad tap him on the shoulder and tell him, "Now, son, let him sleep on it."

The selling process is driven by a series of decisions. The more quickly those decisions are made, the shorter the selling cycle. Jeff was never going to shorten his selling cycle until he became more comfortable getting his prospects to make decisions, and he wasn't going to become more comfortable even asking them to make decisions until he was more comfortable making his own decisions.

To help Jeff with his decision-making challenge, his Sandler Training coach invited him to a lunch meeting at a very nice, very expensive restaurant. The pretense for the meeting was to discuss a strategy for shortening Jeff's selling cycle. "Here are the ground rules for lunch," the coach, who knew Jeff's script, said. "When the waitress comes over, I want you to look at the menu. You'll have thirty seconds to make your selection. I'll be timing you. If you make a selection in thirty seconds or less, I'll pay for lunch. If you take longer than thirty seconds, you'll pay for lunch, and you should know, Jeff, that I'm very, very hungry today. Are you OK with that?" (Notice that the coach's phrase "Are you OK with that?" *modeled* the critical skill of helping another person to make a decision.)

Jeff was puzzled, and even a bit uncomfortable, but he trusted his coach and agreed.

Before calling the waitress over, Jeff's coach asked him to describe the worst-case scenario that could result from making a quick selection. Jeff thought for a moment, and then replied, "I suppose I could end up ordering something that's not as good as something else I could have chosen."

Jeff's coach knew that the one experience **of making a quick lunch decision wasn't going to** rewrite **Jeff's scripted behavior, but it did demonstrate the** *possibility* **of making a good decision without sleeping on it.**

The coach then asked Jeff to describe the best-case scenario.

"I could order something I really enjoy, have a great lunch . . . and you'd pay for it," was Jeff's answer.

"And that's desirable?" the coach asked.

"Absolutely," Jeff answered.

"Now, here is the all-important question," the coach said. "Can you live with the worst-case outcome?"

"I suppose so. It's only one lunch," was Jeff's answer.

The coach called the waitress over, she handed Jeff a menu, and his coach began timing him. Jeff made his selection with twelve seconds to spare.

Jeff confessed that he felt "pressure" making his decision. "Not by the requirement to make a decision," he admitted, "but more by the time constraint—trying to beat the clock."

Jeff's coach knew that the one experience of making a quick lunch decision wasn't going to rewrite Jeff's scripted behavior, but it did demonstrate the *possibility* of making a good decision without sleeping on it. Once Jeff knew it was possible to do this, his attitude changed.

> **Starting with the very first decision, they identified alternative behaviors that would facilitate obtaining the decisions in a timelier manner.**

Jeff worked with his coach to identify the various decisions required to move the selling process from start to finish, and particularly those decision points where Jeff's "sleep on it" script caused him to drag his feet in obtaining a decision from a prospect. Starting with the very first decision, they identified alternative behaviors that would facilitate obtaining the decisions in a timelier manner. They then discussed the best-case and worst-case scenarios of the alternative behaviors, much as they had regarding the lunch-order decision. They discovered that, just as with that decision, the best-case scenarios were desirable, and Jeff could live with the worst-case scenarios.

Jeff made a commitment to implement the new behavior. Like Martha, he was uncomfortable implementing his new behavior at first. Interestingly, though, the worst-case scenarios he had imagined never occurred. His prospects didn't always comply with his wishes; he occasionally received some pushback. Rather than leave the situation open-ended, which he had always done in the past, he was now comfortable asking the prospect to commit to a date by which the decision would be made. Over time, even those situations became rare.

Within ninety days, Jeff cut his selling-cycle time almost in half.

Learning to make good decisions more quickly had a much more profound impact on Jeff, however. In the same period of time, he bought a new car, proposed to his girlfriend (she accepted), and applied for and obtained a new job—all of which were things he had been "sleeping on" for some time.

Jim Searches for Approval

Jim is a salesman working in the financial services arena. He is a people person. He is very outgoing and exudes confidence. His rapport skills are excellent and most people warm up to him very quickly. He thrives on interacting with others. Unlike the vast majority of people who sell for a living, he'd rather be out making cold calls than sitting at a desk doing paperwork!

Jim's colleagues respect him and often ask for his help. His clients like him—many have become personal friends. He earns a very comfortable income. Management often points to his drive and enthusiasm for developing new business as an example for others. By most people's measures, Jim is highly successful; he enjoys his success and the lifestyle it's made possible for him.

> **Jim's Child script would cause him to feel bad if he didn't see constant evidence of approval from those with whom he interacted.**

However, it wasn't always that way. For most of his life, Jim had lived a very different way.

Jim's Child had a high need for approval. The little six-year-old inside didn't merely want to be liked, he *needed* to be liked and accepted, and *needed* to see outward expressions of that acceptance. Jim's Child script would cause him to feel bad if he didn't see constant evidence of approval from those with whom he interacted. He would feel as though he had done something wrong. And, he would feel compelled to make it right, often going overboard. Jim would give you the shirt off his back—literally—if he thought that was appropriate.

His obsessive behavior was a distraction for everyone involved. He could be a real pain in a certain part of the anatomy.

Here's a typical example. If Jim greeted a colleague with an enthusiastic "Good morning," and didn't receive an equally enthusiastic "Good morning" in return, he would immediately assume that his colleague was upset with him, that he had done something wrong or something to offend the person. He couldn't conceive that the person was simply having an off morning or was absorbed in his work. Jim's Child simply couldn't live with the perceived disapproval. In his mind, approval had to be regained, so Jim would bend over backward to make that happen. He would run out and buy donuts or pastries to share with the person. Several times during the day, he would walk past the person's desk and make a complimentary comment or ask a question designed to test the waters—all to determine whether he had regained the perceived lost approval. His obsessive behavior was a distraction for everyone involved. He could be a real pain in a certain part of the anatomy.

As you have probably guessed, Jim's approval needs didn't stop with his colleagues. If a client or prospect cut short a conversation, for instance, Jim's immediate assumption was that he had said or done something to precipitate the action. He would then waste time and energy trying to figure out what to do to fix the imaginary problem. He would send the person e-mail messages with conciliatory language that was not only unnecessary, but also confusing, since the situation he was trying to smooth over existed only in his mind.

Planting his feet with a prospect or client—holding firm on a price, for instance—was another area in which his acceptance needs hurt him. Holding the line on price, from his Child perspective, was a surefire way to lose the person's approval, so he would give in. Asking a prospect or customer to honor a commitment he was attempting to back away from was just as difficult for Jim. The bottom line for Jim was that it was more important for the prospect or customer to like him than it was for him to obtain the business. What he didn't realize was that the two were not mutually exclusive outcomes.

Jim's constant need for approval spilled over into his personal life as well, where its impact was even more damaging. He would constantly seek from his friends not only reassurances of their acceptance of him, but also reassurances that he was a good person—someone worthy of being liked by others. He would recount an experience, such as the "Good morning" incident described above, and then seek assurance that he didn't do anything wrong. His relentless requests put people off and eventually drove many of his loved ones away, including his wife (now his former wife), who eventually had enough and called it quits.

Jim was well aware of his need for approval and the negative impact it had on his life. But, he felt helpless to do anything about it.

Interestingly, Jim was well aware of his need for approval and the negative impact it had on his life. But, he felt helpless to do anything about it. "It's just the way I am," was his explanation. He simply could not imagine feeling or acting differently.

With constant encouragement and support from his Sandler Training coach, Jim made some progress dealing with the debilitating aspects of his Child script as it related to his selling activities. Based on the progress he was making in the sales arena, Jim began to believe that further change was possible, not only in his professional life, but in other areas of his life as well. In this situation, however, no real progress was going to take place without the help of a professional counselor. This was a suggestion Jim had heard many times from friends and relatives. Working with a professional, however, was something he was very reluctant to do.

The wake-up call that made him take a hard look at his life and where it was headed was a question asked by his closest friend, Jack, who was well aware of the negative consequences of Jim's need-for-approval behavior. Jack asked, "Are you happy with your life?"

Jim's answer was a rather apathetic, "It's all right."

Jack told him, "If you're happy living a life that's 'all right' rather than a life that's *great*, or *fulfilling*, or *spectacular*, or *wonderful*, keep doing what you're doing. Don't seek help. But, if you're open to something other than just 'all right,' then you need to see a professional, and I'll help you any way I can."

> **Jim was able to understand that the behavior that had helped him to cope with stressful and uncertain situations as a child . . . was no longer appropriate for his adult interactions.**

At that moment, Jim finally decided to see a psychologist. After just a few weeks, Jim was able to understand that the behavior that had helped him to cope with stressful and uncertain situations as a child—situations such as losing his mother when he was very young, or interacting with the two step-mothers whose love and acceptance he sought for years without success, or the numerous step-siblings he had to deal with, all before reaching his teenage years—was no longer appropriate for his adult interactions.

Over time, with the help of his therapist and the support of his friends, Jim was able to move beyond the feelings that had prompted his approval-seeking behavior and develop new ways of thinking and acting that enabled him to become the successful, confident person he is today.

Bowling Pin Syndrome

In this chapter, I've shared three of the most dramatic stories we (the authors) have encountered to illustrate, in the most compelling ways possible, how three different people overcame what I call the **Bowling Pin Syndrome**. What matters most now, though, is not how these three people learned to move beyond the syndrome of letting outdated beliefs, actions, and behaviors drive their expectations of themselves, but how *you* can move beyond that syndrome.

Each of us has patterns of behavior **that may have worked at some point in our lives but are** not appropriate **to a given sales situation or our current *life* situation.**

What assumptions are you making about yourself and the world around you? What script is driving your behavior and your interactions—right now, today? What expectations about yourself and your capacities has that script built into your life? What is that script costing you, in dollar terms and in human terms? **What is that script telling you that you could be, and how far away is that expectation from what you *can* be once you find a coach who can help you to build, and follow, a better script?**

In «««
Summary

Each of us has patterns of behavior that may have worked at some point in our lives but are not appropriate to a given sales situation or our current *life* situation.

When we were young, we decided to use these behaviors because they were effective or useful in some way.

Starting right now, though, we can recognize that they are getting in our way.

We can decide that they are no longer useful and necessary, and we can get to work on building patterns of behavior that do support us.

Time for
REFLECTION

The New You

What would you change about your behavior?

>> Think about a negative or unproductive behavior pattern you'd like to change.

>> Determine the thinking behind the action. What could be driving the behavior? What early life experiences might have inspired the behavior?

>> Identify an alternative behavior that will serve you better.

>> Identify what you have to gain by making a change.

>> Create a mental image of yourself acting in the new manner, then practice speaking the words that accompany the behavior.

>> Find someone you trust with whom you can rehearse your new behavior, someone who will give you honest feedback about your daily, weekly, and monthly progress in moving away from the old script and creating and following a new script that supports you.

EPILOGUE
The Ultimate Success Principle

Which of the following would you say has the greatest impact on your ultimate selling success and your success in life?

>> The **goals and action plans** you develop and implement.

>> Your **attitude and outlook** about what is possible and what you can accomplish.

>> The **strategies and techniques** you employ.

Please choose one *before* turning the page.

Which of the three did you choose?

Most people think of success in terms of accomplishments, such as winning a major account, reaching sales goals, winning sales awards, or getting promoted. All of these achievements are *signs* of success, and all are the result of the *convergence* of the three core elements you just considered:

» **Behavior**—goals and action plans

» **Attitude**—outlook, beliefs, and expectations

» **Technique**—strategies and tactics

This was a trick question if there ever was one, but it was a trick question weighted in your favor because you were guaranteed to get the right answer. Each of these three elements is connected to the other two; therefore, all three together define truly successful people. Technique alone won't accomplish much if it's not channeled into an appropriate framework of behavior—a plan of action. Even your best plans are doomed to failure if you don't have the confidence to implement the plan and the expectation of a positive outcome.

Study the lives of the most admired and successful people in history, and you will find all three of these elements intersecting in their lives. Study the lives of those who failed to live up to their potential and you will find one, two, or all three of the elements lacking.

All three elements must *converge* if success is to become a reality in anyone's life. You really need all three, and you need all three to work together, so whichever element you chose, you were correct, or at least partially so.

There's a simple way to remember this convergence principle. Think of success as a triangle, with *behavior, attitude,* and *technique* as the three sides of that triangle.

Figure 12.1: Success Triangle

David Sandler taught that, in order for us to reach high levels of success in sales (or in any other calling), *we must continually work on all three of these elements—as a lifetime calling.* It is no exaggeration to describe the three sides of the triangle as the foundation of all enduring personal and professional success.

> **It is no exaggeration to describe the three sides of the triangle as the foundation of all enduring personal and professional success.**

What follows are some brief insights on each element of the Success Triangle. They are offered, not as end points, but as starting points in your own ongoing, lifelong internal dialogue on how best to bring the three elements into convergence in your own life. We'll begin with attitude as our starting point.

Attitude

What comes to mind when you think of the word "attitude"?

Most people associate attitude with being either positive or negative. The *American Heritage Dictionary* defines "attitude" as "A state of mind or feeling with regard to some matter." Since attitudes can and do change, let me suggest that we add the phrase "at any given point in time" to the dictionary definition.

What are the "matters" about which you have a state of mind or feeling that can affect your overall success in the sales arena? They are:

>> yourself

>> your company

>> your product or service

>> your marketplace

Your state of mind or feeling about yourself, your company, your product, and so on can be positive, leading to an outlook of possibility. Alternately, your state of mind can be negative, leading

129

to an outlook of limitation. In other words, you can see all the reasons and ways to make something happen, or you can see all the reasons and obstacles that prevent it from happening. Most of our outlooks are self-imposed.

You really can choose which outlook you will have: one of possibility or one of limitation. The choice you make about your own outlook will inevitably have a greater impact on your success than almost any other choice.

We usually develop our attitudes—both outlooks of possibility and outlooks of limitation—based on a perception we've formed or on an experience. If you are given a task to accomplish or a goal to achieve—usually called a quota by your sales manager—you have some notion of how attainable that goal is, how easy or hard it will be to reach it, or how much time or effort will be required. You might look at the goal and say, "Piece of cake." Or you might say, "No way; it can't be done." The outlook you choose is usually the result of previous experience—yours or someone else's.

> **The choice you make about your own outlook will inevitably have a greater impact on your success than almost any other choice.**

The outlook you choose to hold is the first step in creating a self-fulfilling prophecy.

The actions you take are influenced by the judgments you make, which in turn are based on beliefs that resulted from your original outlook. The result of those actions will serve to reinforce your original outlook—a self-fulfilling prophecy. Whenever you change your outlook, you start a chain reaction that will change your outcome. *If you think you can, you can. If you think you can't, then you can't. Or, worse, you won't even try.*

Behavior

Let's return to the dictionary for a definition of "behavior." There we find the following: "The actions or reactions of persons under specified circumstances."

What are the "circumstances"? They are the salesperson's goals. It's the reason he or she has for doing the daily activity.

Who specifies these circumstances or goals? Well, it should be the salesperson, not some external cause such as a sales quota or the expectations of the salesperson's manager, spouse, or relatives.

> **Goals drive your behavior. They get you out of bed in the morning and motivate you to tackle the day's activities. Goals breathe life and meaning into those activities.**

Salespeople must define their own circumstances—their goals. Once they determine what they want to do, they can develop an action plan for accomplishment.

Let me suggest that the sales goals you set for yourself have roots in other, more personal goals. After all, your life is about more than working and making money. You have personal financial goals that will directly affect the sales goals you set for yourself each month or quarter. If you want to buy a house or take a big vacation, some or all of the money for those goals will come from your income. You also have personal growth goals that motivate you to improve yourself. Those goals have some bearing on your sales goals as well.

Goals drive your behavior. They get you out of bed in the morning and motivate you to tackle the day's activities.

Goals breathe life and meaning into those activities. Without goals, you're only going through the motions, working one day after another waiting for the weekend to roll around again.

Ask yourself:

>> Why do some people carry their goals around in their heads instead of committing them to paper?

>> Why aren't some people specific about their goals?

>> Why are some people hesitant to share their goals?

>> Why do some people have long-term goals but not short-term or daily goals?

>> Why do some people play it safe with their goals by refusing to stretch themselves beyond the level they have already reached?

As you begin to formalize your own goals, be sure to focus on **SMARTER** goals. In other words:

Your goals should be *Specific*. Don't just say you want to earn a lot of money; say exactly how much. If a goal is to grow your client base, indicate how many new clients you will develop.

Your goals should be *Measurable*. You can't track your progress unless your goals are measurable.

Your goals should be *Attainable*. Set goals that make you stretch, yet are attainable. Setting impossible goals will only set you up for failure and de-motivate you.

Why do some people play it safe with their goals by refusing to stretch themselves beyond the level they have already reached?

Your goals should be *Relevant*. Set goals that make sense for you and that relate to your other objectives.

Your goals should be *Time-bound*. Have a time frame for achieving your goals that is appropriate and realistic. Your goal timetable should span the range from daily to short-term (a year or less) to long-term (two, five, or even ten years out). Decide which goals fit into each category. If you give yourself too much time to make goal, you may lose your motivation; too little time makes achieving a goal impossible.

You goals should be *Enjoyable*. How motivated are you likely to be and for how long are you likely to do something you don't enjoy doing? Not very likely and not very long.

> **Unless you find a** more enjoyable **way of** uncovering **new opportunities, the goal is** lost.

Suppose your goal is to increase sales by a certain amount and your plan is to uncover new opportunities by making cold calls. But, you don't enjoy making cold calls. How long will you keep up the activity? Not long. What happens to the goal when your cold-calling activity begins to slide? Technically, you didn't abandon your goal: you still want to increase sales and earn more money. You abandoned the activity that would have enabled you to achieve the goal. Unless you find a more enjoyable way of uncovering new opportunities, the goal is lost. So, make sure your plan of action for goal achievement is enjoyable or, at the very least, includes some enjoyable activities.

Your goals should be *Rewarding*. We've all heard the saying, "achievement is its own reward." That may be true, but unless we celebrate our achievements, our motivation inevitably wanes. Let's suppose that your goal for the year is to increase your income and you have set monthly target amounts to keep you on track. Each month that you hit the number, reward yourself—take your spouse or significant other out to dinner at a special restaurant and celebrate your accomplishment. Make it a ritual you can look forward to.

Once you have set your goals, you will need to develop a plan for achieving them. How many calls do you need to make each day to make your sales goals? Which organizations will you consider joining in order to meet your networking goal? Determine how the necessary activities will fit into your timetable so you can make steady progress toward even your long-term goals.

Build into your plan a method for tracking your progress so you can tell whether you are on schedule for meeting your goals or not.

Keep a journal to track your daily goals. Use a similar method to keep track of the goal-related activities you are doing and plan to check up on yourself periodically.

Technique

The word "technique," in the context of the Success Triangle, simply refers to the tools by which salespeople implement their behavior planning. Your technique comprises your **strategies** and your **tactics**.

Strategies are the plans you use to achieve a goal during the selling process. For example, if your goal is to qualify or disqualify a prospect, the strategy defined by the Sandler Selling System is to uncover the prospect's pain, budget issues, and decision-making process.

> Mastering a technique involves more than rote memorization of a pattern.

Tactics are the actual "moves" you make to carry out your strategy, such as asking particular questions in a particular sequence and manner. Delivering a thirty-second commercial at the beginning of a prospecting call is another example of a tactic—in this case, one that carries out the strategy of engaging the prospect in a conversation.

Mastering a technique involves more than rote memorization of a pattern. For one thing, you are not alone in the process, and the other person will not always follow your memorized pattern. As a result, every situation is different and requires a slightly different application of your technique. To use a technique effectively, you must:

» understand the situation you're facing.

» know which skill to use in that situation and why.

» know and be able to apply the skill in that situation.

» be willing to "give it a try," knowing full well that your application may not be flawless, and that each "flawed" attempt is an opportunity to learn and improve your skill.

Synergy = Success

Getting all three elements of the Success Triangle to *converge* on a regular basis is, as I have said, a long-term project. The reward for undertaking that project is the special synergy that is created by the three converging elements of the Success Triangle.

> **Getting all three elements of the Success Triangle to *converge* on a regular basis is a long-term project.**

Reaching the highest levels of success is largely the function of these three elements working in concert. Learning a new prospecting approach (technique), for instance, won't ensure you of more business unless you have a plan for implementing that approach (behavior), and the belief (attitude) that it will work for you.

If attitude plus behavior plus technique equals "success," and I firmly believe it does, then what is the long-term result when any one of the three elements is missing in our lives? Consider the following possibilities:

Attitude + Behavior - Technique = Working hard: can be discouraging and de-motivating

Attitude + Technique - Behavior = Working frantically, without clear goals: can lead to burnout

Behavior + Technique - Attitude = Going through the motions: leaves one stuck in mediocrity

In Closing . . .

The Success Triangle takes just a few minutes to understand . . . and a lifetime to master. Once you recognize how these three seemingly simple elements support everything else you have learned here, once you begin to evaluate where you are now and where you want to be on each element of the triangle, once you accept the challenge of working on all three of the elements *continuously*—starting with this moment and continuing for the rest of your life—you will realize that this really is the ultimate success principle. You will begin noticing that virtually every system, philosophy, or program designed to inspire, promote, or support personal and professional success makes some use of what you've just learned.

> **You will know for certain that you are trying to implement the Success Triangle in your own life when you begin to put it into your own terms, in a way that makes sense to you personally.**

The Success Triangle can be reformulated, elaborated upon, and reexamined in any number of ways. You will know for certain that you are trying to implement the Success Triangle in your own life when you begin to put it into your own terms, in a way that makes sense to you personally.

Here is an example of how one of the most successful "graduates" of the Sandler program adapted the Success Triangle in his own life and for those he counsels:

> Behaviors are goals in action. They're the things you're willing to do every day, every week, that make you a good prospector, a good salesperson, a good manager. They're the things that make you successful in your career, the things that build your character, the things that make you a winner in life. What new behaviors—what new habits— are you building for yourself right now to grow old with?

This is clear evidence of an ongoing, lifelong *engagement with the Success Triangle*, and it's this kind of engagement I'm hoping you, too, will take from the principles David Sandler created to make success a reality in selling . . . and in life. My hope is not just that you understand his material, but that you engage with it, implement it, and live it to the high level that his very best students have.

GLOSSARY

A

Adult Ego State: The ego state oriented toward objective, autonomous data processing and probability estimating; direct responses to the here and now (*see also* Child Ego State; Ego State; Parent Ego State)

After-Burn: Worry about a previous or past event; the situation in which thoughts about a past event are carried forward and have a negative impact on your current behavior (*see also* Reach-Back)

At-Leasters: People who rate their Identity between four and six; their Identity rating is closely tied to their role performance; they don't stretch outside their comfort zone to strive for greater levels of success (*see also* I/R Theory; Losers; Transactional Analysis; Winners)

Attitude: A state of mind or feeling with regard to some matter at any given point in time; outlook, beliefs, and expectations (*see also* Behavior; Success Triangle; Technique)

B

Behavior: The actions or reactions of persons under specified circumstances; goals and action plans (*see also* Attitude; Success Triangle; Technique)

Bowling Pin Syndrome: The syndrome of letting outdated beliefs, actions, and behaviors drive personal expectations

C

Child Ego State: The ego state in which feelings in response to external events (mostly input from parents and parent figures) between birth and the age of five are recorded; a felt concept of life (*see also* Adult Ego State; Ego State; Parent Ego State)

Critical Parent: The compartment of the Parent Ego State in which parental directives—rules and limits—are stored (*see also* Adult Ego State; Child Ego State; Ego State; Nurturing Parent; Parent Ego State)

E

Ego State: A pattern of feeling and experience directly related to a corresponding consistent pattern of behavior (*see also* Adult Ego State; Child Ego State; Critical Parent; Nurturing Parent; Parent Ego State)

Emotional Motivation: Stimulus for action derived from feelings rather than from a logical or factual base

F

Fear: Worry or anxiety about an event or situation (*see also* Scare)

I

I/R Theory: Differentiates between identity and roles to help people understand the interconnected nature of these two concepts

L

Life Script: An unconscious decision made in childhood about how life should be lived that is reinforced by parents and justified by subsequent events

Losers: People who consistently rate their Identity somewhere between zero and three; they have low self-esteem and tend to have little confidence in their abilities and judgment (*see also* At-Leasters; I/R Theory; Transactional Analysis; Winners)

N

Nurturing Parent: The compartment of the Parent Ego State in which advice and guidance (primarily to protect and nurture the Child) are stored (*see also* Adult Ego State; Child Ego State; Critical Parent; Ego State; Parent Ego State)

O

OK Emotions: Emotions that make us feel OK—confident, content, etc.

P

Parent Ego State: Behaviors, thoughts, and feelings copied from parents or parent figures (*see also* Adult Ego State; Child Ego State; Critical Parent; Ego State; Nurturing Parent)

Perceptiveness: The ability to see clearly and intuitively into the nature of a complex person, situation, or subject

R

Reach-Back: Worry about a future event; the situation in which thoughts about a future event "reach back" and have a negative impact on your current behavior (*see also* After-Burn)

S

Scare: A situation causing alarm (*see also* Fear)

Script: A pattern of behavior derived from childhood experiences and decisions

Self-Awareness: Having a balanced and honest view of your own personality and often an ability to interact with others frankly and confidently

Self-Worth: Confidence in personal value and worth as an individual person

Strategies: The plans you use to achieve a goal (*see also* Tactics; Technique)

Success Triangle: A visual and symbolic representation of the convergence of the three core components of success: Attitude, Behavior, and Technique (*see also* Attitude; Behavior; Technique)

T

Tactics: The actual "moves" you make to carry out your strategy (*see also* Strategies; Technique)

Technique: Refers to the tools by which people implement their behavior planning; strategies and tactics (*see also* Behavior; Strategies; Success Triangle; Tactics)

Transactional Analysis: A theory of personality, communication, and behavior that describes and predicts the interactions between individuals

W

Winners: People who consistently rate their Identity between seven and ten; they have high self-esteem and feel good about themselves regardless of the outcome of their role experiences (*see also* At-Leasters; I/R Theory; Losers; Transactional Analysis)

If you like SANDLER SUCCESS PRINCIPLES...
You may amplify the insights you've gained by reading our bestselling companion book:

THE SANDLER RULES: *49 Timeless Selling Principles and How to Apply Them*

Here's a preview of just a few of the Sandler Rules:

Don't spill your candy in the lobby.

Never answer an unasked question.

When prospecting, go for the appointment.

Money does grow on trees.

A prospect who is listening is no prospect at all.

Never ask for the order – make the prospect give up.

Don't paint "seagulls" in your prospect's picture.

Sell today, educate tomorrow.

Product knowledge at the wrong time can be intimidating.

People buy in spite of the hard sell, not because of it.

You can't sell anybody anything – they must
discover they want it.

You can't lose anything you don't have.

Get an I.O.U. for everything you do.

If your competition does it, stop doing it right away.

The problem the prospect brings you is
never the real problem.

When your foot hurts, you're probably standing
on your own toe.

Express your feelings through third-party stories.

Selling is a Broadway play performed
by a psychiatrist.

Excerpted from THE SANDLER RULES: 49 Timeless Selling Principles and How to Apply Them
By David Mattson
ISBN 9780982255483

PEGASUS
Media World

2009

SANDLERSUCCESSPRINCIPLES.COM